C000246489

THE OPEN PATH

THE
OPEN PATH

Recognizing Nondual Awareness

ELIAS AMIDON

SENTIENT PUBLICATIONS

First Sentient Publications edition 2012
Copyright © 2012 by Sufi Way Ltd.

All rights reserved. This book, or parts thereof, may not be reproduced in any form
without permission, except in the case of brief quotations embodied in critical articles
and reviews.

A paperback original

Cover design by Kim Johansen, Black Dog Design, www.blackdogdesign.com
Book design by Timm Bryson

Library of Congress Cataloging-in-Publication Data
Amidon, Elias.
  The open path : recognizing nondual awareness / Elias Amidon. -- 1st
Sentient Publications ed.
    p. cm.
  Includes bibliographical references.
  ISBN 978-1-59181-179-4
  1. Awareness--Religious aspects. 2. Spiritual life. I. Title.
  BL629.5.A82A45 2012
  204'.4--dc23
                                    2012026761

Printed in the United States of America

10 9 8 7 6 5 4 3 2 1

SENTIENT PUBLICATIONS
A Limited Liability Company
1113 Spruce Street
Boulder, CO 80302
www.sentientpublications.com

To Rabia

Contents

PREFACE

This book is a guide for awakening to the spontaneous presence of awareness that is our most intimate nature and the silent ground of all being. It is meant for anyone committed to realizing this awakening now, and for learning to sustain and express it in the diverse conditions of one's daily life.

I originally wrote this book as a manual to accompany the nine-month Open Path trainings that are currently held in the United Kingdom, the Netherlands, Germany, and the United States. During the trainings, these written teachings are supplemented by three residential seminars, frequent telephone conferencing, and individual guidance. While such personal and small-group contact is ideal for this work, many Open Path students encouraged me to publish this course material on its own for a wider audience. The result of their encouragement is the book you now hold in your hands.

I have kept the style of this book close to the original course manual, trusting that those who are drawn to it would want to engage this subject as whole-heartedly as the students of the nine-month trainings. One of the best ways to do this may be to read this book with a friend or a group of friends, discussing passages that are of mutual interest and sharing the exercises. Otherwise, if you are reading this book on your own you may find it helpful to read through the text slowly, even rereading portions of it several times. It may also help for you to become familiar with a number of the books suggested in the bibliography, reading them with the same attention as you do this book. It is good to explore the direct recognition of nondual awareness from a number of traditions and styles of expression.

In addition, many of the chapters here include exercises and practices. It is easy to skim over these thinking you'll get to them later, or that by simply reading them you get their point and don't need to explore them more deeply. Sometimes this may be so, but more often you may find that by taking the time to do an exercise — and by maintaining a daily practice of calming your mind and simplifying your activities — a sense of equanimity and natural insight will arise.

However, I encourage you not to make studying the material in this book and engaging with these practices a pressure or something that you must discipline yourself to do. The gentle fact that you now hold this book in your hands is evidence that awakening to the spontaneous presence of awareness is already welcoming itself in your life. You don't have to do anything with effort here; just open to it as it naturally arises in you. Do as little or as much study and practice as you feel to do. Of course, the more you open to it in your life the more it will welcome you. But don't worry about outcomes. Direct recognition of timeless awareness is not something you attain through striving for it. It is already present and is the very nature of your being now.

My hope is that at least some of the teachings and practices here will help make possible for you a synchronistic recognition of the clear light of timeless awareness. I use the word "synchronistic" because in actuality recognition of the spontaneous presence of nondual awareness is not transmittable *from* someone *to* someone. The transparent light of awareness that is the ever-present ground of being can only be pointed to, although in truth there is no direction toward which one may reliably point. Even to describe it as "transparent light," or "presence," or "nondual awareness," or "it," misses the mark. Nothing that can be said can adequately represent this that is simultaneously present and absent, immanent and transcendent, and in fact beyond any dimension in which these kinds of polarities make sense. It does not yield to conceptualization. And even more to the point, no guaranteed formula leads to its recognition. In the end, recognition is a matter of synchronistic grace. Yet it *is* possible to "put yourself in the way of it," as the Sufi mystic Ibn al'Arabi remarked. That is the purpose of this book.

A NOTE ABOUT THE SOURCES OF THE OPEN PATH

The approach of the Open Path as represented in this book has been profoundly shaped by my forty years of Sufi training, along with extensive study of other mystical traditions. An acknowledgement of these sources can be found at the back of this book.

Consequently, the methods and practices of the Open Path have been drawn from many different sources: classical and modern Sufi practices and teachings; contemporary psychological methods for releasing mental and emotional fixations; meditation practices from various traditions; forms of inquiry from Zen, Advaita Vedanta, and Tibetan Dzogchen and Mahamudra traditions; and from the teachings of many historic and contemporary Western nondual teachers.

The approach of the Open Path is inclusive. It does not claim to be original, and it borrows freely from many other traditions and teachers. I acknowledge these here with profound gratitude for their priceless gifts.

· 1 ·

OPEN AWARENESS

Awareness is primordial; it is the original state, beginningless, end-less, uncaused, unsupported, without parts, without change...It is the common matrix of every experience.[1]

SRI NISARGADATTA MAHARAJ (C.1960)

One of the most joyful moments in the life of the spiritual seeker is when seeking finally ends: when we recognize that the long sought-for goal of the spiritual quest is already present within us as our natural awareness. We recognize that *what we seek, we are* — this transparent, pure awareness at the center of our being is a clear window into oneness. With this recognition comes the realization that nothing more needs to be done. Nothing needs to change. We don't have to improve ourselves. Each one of us is already worthy of illu-mined awareness because it is our innate nature. This realization opens in us an indescribable sense of relief and freedom from self-judgment. We understand in these moments of realization that we are completely one with all of reality and have always been so, and that this natural state is utterly safe, free, kind, and radiant with a

supernal beauty. We don't have to do anything to make this be true. It does it all by itself.

The central purpose of the Open Path is simply to become familiar with opening into this fundamental realization of what is already true — learning how to relax into and stabilize this recognition of our innate nature, what I often call "open awareness" or simply "awareness."

WHAT IS OPEN AWARENESS?

This question is at the heart of our work together. We will use many words and exercises to focus on this question, so that, again and again, we can look directly into what it asks. But the answer that comes will not have anything to do with words. Each of us must leave behind words and thoughts to allow space for the answer to arise. It will appear intuitively to us, from the inside out. In fact, it will not even "appear" like an image or thought appears in our awareness, because here we are asking awareness to be aware of itself.

This is asking the impossible: awareness can no more be aware of itself than our eye can see itself. Why? First of all, awareness is not a thing or an object of any kind. It has no shape or color. It is completely transparent and invisible. What is more, it cannot be felt or sensed in any way that would reveal awareness to us as something knowable *out there*. And yet we know we are aware, we know awareness *is*. Awareness is the foundation of everything we have ever experienced or will experience. Every object, every thought, every emotion, every sensation, every memory is known because it appears in awareness. *Otherwise it could not be known.* Awareness is the root of our entire sense of existence, and yet where is it? What is it? How can it be apprehended? We know it *is*, but whenever we try to look directly into awareness we see...*nothing!*

This is a clue. Awareness is not a thing. We might say it is nothing, but is it simply nothing? It is awareness! Whatever it is, it never takes substantial form. It is, as Buddhists might say, empty of substantiality. It is open. It has no edges. It is spaciousness itself. It is boundless, yet somehow utterly present. What is more, it is lucid: completely clear and at the same time light-bearing, i.e., "the light of awareness."

Throughout this book we will return repeatedly to this question of what open awareness is — and we will invite ourselves to investigate the question originally, for ourselves, not in the abstract but directly and experientially. In fact, you are encouraged to do that right now. Notice, as you read this, that you are aware of the words being used, the thoughts they evoke, the shape of the letters, the white of the paper or screen on which they are written, a few things seen peripherally in the room where you read this, the sense of your body sitting where it is. These are all perceptions appearing in "your" awareness. They can be seen, felt, or sensed.

But what can you say about the awareness that is aware of them? Look as deeply and as steadily as you can. Become familiar with that looking, as if you were turning 180 degrees around from looking out of your eyes and now are looking inwardly at what is looking. What do you "see?" Explore this on your own, as often as you can. Here's a hint: if you look *for* something, you will be disappointed. Instead, simply allow yourself to relax from all "looking" and simply "see" without trying to uncover some discovery. Relax. While awareness cannot be aware of awareness, it can *be* it. It *is* it, naturally.

Some say it is helpful at this point to shift your sense of looking *for* something with your eyes or your intellect and allow your heart to *open to* the question "What is awareness?" By "heart" I mean the whole presence of awareness in which intellect, sensations, and emotions appear. This is what Sufis call *al 'ayn al qalb* — "the eye of the heart." It is the whole of awareness as it is experienced through your body. Open to the presence of awareness with your whole heart.

A NOTE ABOUT THE WORDS USED HERE

In these pages I will use many names to signify this indescribable, but definitely recognizable, reality that is the sublime ground of all being. These diverse names, drawn from spiritual traditions throughout the world, indicate both this primal reality and our capacity to recognize it: *nondual awareness, pure awareness, open awareness, presence-awareness, unconditioned mind, rigpa, primordial experience, This, the basic state, the sublime, buddha nature, original nature, spontaneous presence, the oneness of being, the ground of being, the Real, clarity, God-consciousness, divine light, the clear light, illumination, realization,* and *enlightenment.*

These terms refer to the reality that countless seekers throughout history have inquired into, meditated on, experienced, and spoken about. However it is expressed, these labels point to the ultimate goal of all human desire for fulfillment, happiness, and belonging, and the goal of all spiritual searching: the recognition that we are essentially indivisible from what Sufis call the "shoreless ocean" of unconditioned awareness and love.

In this chapter, and often throughout the book, I refer simply to "open awareness" and "awareness" as a name for this fresh, ever-present reality, because these words are relatively free of religious connotations and point to a more directly experienced reality than, say, the words "enlightenment" or "realization." In this way, our ordinary, intimate sense of being aware gives us an entry into experiencing timeless being, free from concepts. The modifier "open" indicates that this is boundless awareness itself, utterly contentless, empty, and unaffected by whatever phenomena show up in it, just as what is reflected in a mirror does not affect the mirror.

But the phrase "open awareness" is not perfect. By calling something "open" — or by using almost any adjective — its opposite is implied, while what we are referring to has no opposite. In addition, for many people the phrase "open awareness" — or simply "awareness" — does not carry a sufficient resonance of the divine, however that may be interpreted. However, rather than getting caught up in these objections, my hope is that throughout this book you will become skillful at going beyond the limits of the various words used, and allow what they signify to open in your heart.

The problem is that language is fundamentally dualistic. It is continually affirming, denying, or comparing the worth of one thing against another. In addition, its subject-predicate structure can't help but reinforce the subject-object polarity that situates us as separate entities negotiating our way through a world of separate objects. The use of pronouns is another good example of the dualistic nature of our language. However convenient they are, the pronouns "I," "you," "he," "she," "me," "mine," etc., imply discrete things or identities that actually exist. Another linguistic problem is how we use prepositions. For example, when we say *rest in natural great peace,* there is an implied topography: something rests *in* something else; once again we are locating discrete somethings in space in relation to each other, while what is seeking expression has nothing to do with either location or "thingness."

However, if we tried to avoid all language that could be interpreted dualistically, we would end up with a poor tool for the job at hand. So in the pages that follow I do not try to stay away from pronouns, or prepositions, or words that can be interpreted dualistically. I do, however, often modify or redefine words, or put them in quotation marks, or point out their limitations while still using them, trusting that you will let them do their work — however provisionally they manage to do so. In any case, if we are lucky, the words — and methods — used in this book will finally fall away as the natural truth becomes clear.

One final point about language: when we use descriptive words and phrases to refer to a reality that is the "ultimate goal of human desire," it is very easy to make this goal seem unattainable to mere mortals like us. Most religions and mystical traditions throughout history have reinforced this notion of a gap between ordinary humans and sublime wisdom. To some extent each of us has inherited the view that enlightenment is far from us. One of the central aims of the Open Path is to free ourselves from this fixation, since it is nothing more than an idea. Pure awareness, enlightenment, awakening, realization, is our birthright — in fact we already *are* it. We don't have to do anything to achieve it. The truth is, we are already doing way too much, both outwardly and inwardly, and that very "doing" is what stands in the way of our recognizing this present, spacious, invisibly radiant nature imminent in our very being, and in the existence of everything.

THE UNCONDITIONED
AND THE CONDITIONED

As you may have already noticed, we have begun to make a distinction between open awareness, which is *contentless,* and the diverse phenomena which are the ordinary *contents* of awareness. This is identical to the distinction between what is called "the unconditioned" and "the conditioned." In later chapters we will address how to recognize and release the limitations of our conditioned mind so that we may open to unconditioned pure awareness. In effect, we will point to what may at first sound like an "absolute realm" of open awareness that is different from the "relative realm" of conditioned life. This distinction is a pedagogical device that is essential in the early stages of our work. While it could be argued that emphasizing a polarity like this is antithetical to the very essence of nondual awareness, I believe it can be helpful to make the distinction to begin with — to pull these two aspects of our experience apart so we can be freed from confusion about them. In the later phases of our work together we will see how everyday conditioned experience and pure, unconditioned, open awareness are inseparable.

This apparent polarity between the unconditioned and the conditioned is famous throughout all religious and spiritual traditions. We see it in the archetypes of God and Lucifer, the sacred and the profane, the absolute and the relative, heaven and earth, nirvana and samsara, the infinite and the finite, the one and the many, the eternal and the mortal, and so on. An important rationale for "pulling these two apart" is to challenge our habitual assumptions about the singular reality of our conditioned, everyday experience and recognize the transparent ground in which all experience arises.

We are all appearing as human beings whose body-minds are the result of an infinite history of apparent conditions leading to our physical existence in this moment. We cannot escape this conditionality. We cannot escape the karma that produced our body-minds in time and space. This vast field of apparent conditions is so complex and unknowable we can only stand in awe that we are here in this form at all.

However, attaching oneself to a particular identity as a personal "I" in the infinite sea of conditions is the source of enormous suffering. Imagine, for example, a fifteen year-old girl who hates herself because she thinks she isn't as pretty or as popular as her classmates. This belief about her identity exists because of many conditions — her culture and social status, her genetic inheritance, her religion, her particular education, her family life, etc. Seeking to know who she is, she sees her reflection in all these conditions and believes her

interpretation of them is accurate. This is "self-referencing awareness" or conditioned mind.

The conditioned mind believes in an entity, a *me*, that needs to
get what it wants and avoid what it doesn't want to be happy. A complex field of likes and dislikes, of hopes and fears, swarms around the
idea of a *me*, making the *me* seem substantial and existent.
Our identification with this *me* is at the root of our discontent and
suffering.

Throughout this book we will be working in many ways to see
through the constructions — the conditioning — we hold about
our identity, those formations which, like those of the fifteen year-
old girl, keep us thinking we are what we are not. Deconstructing
our long-established assumptions and mental and emotional conditioning is not always comfortable, but it is entirely possible, and not
as difficult as we might think. We tend to consider our various personal fixations as having a concrete reality when in fact they have no
substance at all. When faced clearly and steadily they vanish like
snow falling on water.

This "vanishing," so to speak, is the spontaneous presence of the
unconditioned in the midst of the conditioned. Everything we believe to be true is conditioned. Releasing our grasp on our beliefs,
we open to the clarity of unconditioned, self-occurring awareness.

PARADOX

I also want to point to the use of frequent paradoxical expressions
in our work together. "Paradox" in this context is a collision of language that helps break the dualistic, subject-object arrangement of
thought and language that defines our everyday world and our assumptions about it. Paradox appears when two opposing statements
both assert to be true. Their collision momentarily short-circuits the
usual assumptions of thought, and in that gap a flash of the Real
may be experienced.

For example, as I mentioned earlier, we may find ourselves "experiencing" the openness of awareness as nothing. And indeed, open awareness *is* nothing. But it is also awareness. How can it be "nothing" and "aware" at the same time? Since open awareness is seemingly a "state" we have named and can think about, it is easy to treat it as one more thing. But it is not a thing, or a state. In fact, it is empty of any conditions or attributes. The spontaneous presence of unconditioned, open awareness has no limits or boundaries. It is not personal to us, though it is the essence of our being. One analogy is that awareness can be imagined to be like space itself — unlimited, without beginning or end, empty by nature yet allowing all phenomena to arise within it. And like space, awareness is wide open — meaning that it is without content, free of structure, free of conditions, free of the personal self. Its openness pervades all things. *It is not a thing but it pervades all things.* When descriptions approach this kind of paradox they begin to break the confines of language and point to a different order of understanding.

We find the same attempt at expressing the paradoxical co-arising of "the one and the all" in the work of the great Sufi master Ibn ʿArabi:[2]

> How can I know This when It is the inwardly Hidden that is
> not known?
> How can I not know This when It is the outwardly Manifest
> that makes Itself known to me in every thing?
>
> How can I realize Its Unity when in Uniqueness I have no existence?
> How can I not realize Its Unity when Union is the very secret
> of servanthood?
>
> Glory be to This! There is nothing but This!
> Nothing else than This can realize Its Unity, since It is as It is
> in pre-eternity without beginning and in post-eternity

without end. In reality, nothing other than This can realize Its Unity, and in sum, none knows This except This.

It hides and It manifests — yet It does not hide from Itself nor does It manifest to other than Itself, for This is This, there is nothing but This.
How is this paradox to be resolved, when the First is Last and the Last is First?

Because of the paradoxical nature of reality — its simultaneous *thingness* and *no-thingness* — it will sometimes be useful in our work to use conflicting statements, or to correct a previous statement with a qualifier that may seem to contradict the first. This mental ping-pong can sometimes help to tire the mind into relaxing its insistence on seeing things logically. When that happens our obsession with meaning falls away and we begin to see in a new light.

Although paradox may best describe the experience of open awareness, it is, nevertheless, an unmistakable experience. It is precise, yet at the same time this "experience" is free of all structures and attributes. At first we may catch only the quickest glimpse of this "it" we are speaking of. Though the spontaneous presence of open awareness is omnipresent, our capacity to rest in it is limited by our mental reflexes that want to resist its voiding of our sense of self. But through the reminders and practices you will engage in throughout this work, you will be encouraged to return again and again to this glimpse. Gradually the glimpses will get longer and we will develop more comfort to rest in unconfined, uncontrived, pure awareness.

As one Tibetan teacher described this process, it is like ringing a bell. We touch for a moment the experience of empty awareness and it is like striking a little bell. It resonates in us and if we do nothing, the sound continues until it naturally vanishes. But if we strike the bell of empty awareness and then react sharply, saying "Oh! That's it! Oh, where is it?" it is like trying to hit the bell again and again, which only muffles the tone.

In our recognition, we learn to strike the bell and let the tone continue for as long as it naturally does. When it vanishes, then we strike it again — which means we welcome it without effort on our part — and let it be. Gradually the tone increases in duration and we learn to rest naturally in its openness, silence, and ease.

Exercises: Open Awareness

Find a place where you can be alone and undisturbed for at least twenty minutes. Sit comfortably with your back relatively vertical without being stiff. Breathe naturally. Your eyes may be open or closed; you may wish to explore these exercises sometimes with your eyes open, sometimes closed.

1. Gravity and Awareness

Rest in your natural, lucid, alert yet relaxed state of mind. When thoughts, feelings, or sensations arise in your awareness, just let them be without resisting them or following them.

Now notice the sensations of gravity on your body. Allow your attention to notice the pressure of your body on your chair or cushion, the weight of your feet on the floor, your hands in your lap, etc. Now center your attention on one of these sensations.

Next, very gently, ask yourself: what is it that is aware of this sensation? Try to ask this in a way that is not looking for a verbal answer, but rather for a felt sense of the answer. Feel the answer directly. Open to the first-hand experience of "what is aware," rather than an idea about it.

You will find it is helpful not to be aggressive about this inquiry — opening yourself to "what is aware" rather than peering into the unknown looking for something to show itself.

2. Attributes of Awareness

Proceeding from the above exercise, or at a different time, center again on one of the steady sensations in your body that is a sign of gravity — for example, the pressure of your body on your chair or cushion.

Ask again gently: what is it that is aware of this sensation? Once you find that you have a direct intuition of "this that is aware," ask the following questions, giving time to explore the felt sense of your "answers." Go very slowly, take all the time you need.

- Does this awareness have an outer edge or boundary by which I can tell what it is?
- Does this awareness have a color by which I can tell what it is?
- Does this awareness have a texture by which I can tell what it is?
- Does it have a front and a back? A top or a bottom?
- Does this awareness have a center, a "point" of origination by which it can be distinguished?
- Can you find somewhere where the awareness isn't, someplace beyond it?
- Can you find any difference between this that is aware of the sensation of gravity and "you?" If so, what is that difference?

In exploring this inquiry on your own, you may find that you cannot find an edge, a color, a texture, a front and back, a center, someplace beyond, or some difference between you and "it." If this is what occurs for you, simply rest in that unfindability.

If you *can* find an edge, a color, a texture, a front and back, a center, someplace beyond, or some difference between you and "it," then look carefully at that which you find and ask: what is it that is carefully looking? Does it have an edge, a color, a texture, a front or back, a center, someplace beyond, and is there some difference between "you" and "it?"

THE PRACTICE OF SUBTLE OPENING

This chapter introduces a practice — *the practice of subtle opening* — that you may find helpful during this initial stage of our work. Try making it part of your daily routine for the next few months. Ten to fifteen minutes a day may be enough, although you may find you want to do the last part of the practice for longer periods.

One purpose of this practice is simply to calm the mind. The intention here is to help reduce the density and speed of thoughts and emotions that flood our awareness, as well as to relax our identification with the content of these thoughts and emotions. A further purpose is to become familiar with the experience of inner relaxation and spaciousness that accompanies a calmer mind.

While there can be immediate benefit from no longer feeling at the mercy of our "monkey mind," this is not why we do these practices. By working with these practices we are not trying to stop all thoughts from arising. Having a quiet mind is not equivalent to "awakening to open awareness." One can awaken to the clear light of awareness and still have thoughts arise, just as one can still see the myriad colors and textures of the world, or still hear the profusion of sounds of the world.

It is important to recognize that in the Open Path we are not declaring war on our thoughts. We let our thoughts be, as they are. We simply learn to take less interest in them. This disinterestedness has the effect of calming our mental environment. In this calmer environment we may have a better chance to relax into the open clarity in which thoughts, sensations, and emotions appear. This clarity is awareness itself, open and transparent.

Another purpose of the practice of subtle opening is to relax the objectifying habits of our minds. For example, if we speak of subtlety as a quality — what Sufis call *latif* — we might think of it as a quality of lightness, spaciousness, and refinement. As we describe it in this way it already has the tendency to become slightly objectified, turning "subtlety" into a conceptual something that is in some way substantial. Part of our work at this point is to begin to recognize how we do that, how we objectify direct experience into concepts and stories. Once this is seen, we can more easily relax from this objectifying tendency, allowing instead the invocation of subtlety to be a gentle dynamic of opening into openness. This is an important "skill" and central to our work. (I put quotation marks around the word "skill" here because while it is indeed something we can become good at, at the same time it is not something we "do." We relax into subtlety.)

Why subtlety? Because the truth we seek — which is already here — cannot be possessed. We will never find it by seeking. It is not a thing. It is nothing. In itself it is neither subtle nor coarse. And as I have mentioned, to call it an "it" is already betraying it. It is transparent, without center or edge. Yet it is precise; when you "experience" it (another awkward word), you are absolutely certain. It is self-evident. Opening to this transparent self-evidence is aided by an intimate appreciation of what is signified by the word *subtlety*.

THE CONTRADICTION OF PRACTICING

As we begin this work together and start talking about and engaging in practices, we need to acknowledge the contradiction at the center of the idea of practicing. Indeed, it is the contradiction at the center of the Open "Path" itself. The contradiction is this: that which we seek to recognize — our original nature — doesn't require the accomplishment of any practice. In fact, all practices substitute some level of conceptualization for the reality of our true nature. At the same time, we recognize we are hypnotized by mental and emotional identifications and beliefs that obscure realization of our true nature, and these identifications need to be released. To cultivate this release we engage in various practices designed for this purpose, and these constitute a "path." Yet practices — as we have noted — tend to introduce more layers of conceptualization and identification...etc.

In our work we will repeatedly face this contradiction, since it is at the heart of what we are doing together. At this point, we might best proceed by *simply engaging all practices and exercises sincerely but lightly*. Some people build up an attitude about practices and approach their "practice time" with a great deal of effort or expectations of results. Then they judge themselves for "not doing it right" and stop doing the practices altogether.

You might think of the *practice of subtle opening* — and all the practices and exercises in this book — as similar to practicing scales on a musical instrument. Do them with care and with a light heart. Over time they will help give you more ease with this beautiful instrument, your mind. On this path we are learning to open, not close down.

EXPECTING NOTHING

Since our mind stream is well conditioned to constructing subject-object duality in our moment-to-moment experience, most of us need to practice the opposite to relax from this habit. We expect that what we are seeking — pure, contentless awareness — will somehow be recognizable in the same way we recognize all the other objects or things in our experience. We expect it to be something "out there" (an object) perceived by something "in here" (a subject). It is this expectation that keeps us anticipating something that can never appear as something. We must learn to expect nothing. Perhaps even more accurately, *we must learn not to expect*. What we are looking for is already here.

Many of you reading this may have had glimpses of the unconditioned nature of pure awareness. Others may have experienced more prolonged periods of it. More common are experiences of open awareness that are lightly structured — that is, they include perceptions of calmness and feelings of wellbeing, serenity, or elation. While these feelings are wonderful and are surely to be enjoyed, we must be clear with ourselves that they are feelings, not direct recognition of nondual contentless awareness. This doesn't mean we have to push these feelings away, however. Just like more uncomfortable fixations, we simply need to notice them for what they are and notice the flowing of their energy.

We are in the initial stages of learning how to recognize and sustain the realization of unconditioned awareness, which, as we have noted, is not a thing that can be recognized in the same way we recognize things, thoughts, feelings, or other energy events in our mind stream. No-thingness, emptiness, openness, transparence cannot be seen or imagined. This that we seek is known by its absence. It is because it isn't.

When we close our eyes and sit in meditation we often use forms of mantra, *zikr*, "breathing prayers" or *vipassana* labeling exercises to calm our mental activity and achieve a level of serenity. The words that we repeat silently or aloud arise in our awareness as objects or events. We witness them. We, as subject, witness or perceive these mental phenomena as objects of consciousness. When we experience more emotive levels of prayer, we experience feelings such as longing, praise, or gratitude, and these too arise in our awareness as energy events that we witness. They are objects to our subject. When we do nothing at all and are momentarily free from thoughts or feelings, we still may sit in this habitual subject-object mental frame. It may be that we simply experience the muted retinal displays behind our eyelids — objects to our subject — or we experience the composite sense of bodily presence, the feeling of gravity, the light feeling of clothes against our skin, the small aches or pressures of bodily life — all these arise in our awareness as objects in relation to our subjective sense of self.

It is useful to recognize this almost constant dynamic of subject-object distinction and dependence. Notice how it seems to pervade our entire existence. Remember, it is not anything "bad" that we are trying to do away with. Subject-object discrimination is an essential survival skill — without it we would have been food for lions long ago. But for most of us it is the only way we experience the world, a condition that leads to ignorance and suffering. In opening to nondual awareness we don't have to worry that we will lose our ability to discriminate one thing from another, or become a lion's next meal. We are well practiced in this discriminating skill. Our intention is simply to develop — alongside the perception of subject-object dualities — a nondual way of perceiving. We do this by recognizing and resting in the clarity of unconditioned awareness.

The key point here is simply to release all expectation — to let go of anticipating that timeless awareness will appear in any way similar to the way the objects and experiences of our lives appear to us. This is why we invoke subtlety, because subtlety releases expectation: it frees us from our tendency to assert and define. In one sense we could say that our natural state *is* subtlety — boundless, fresh, and without conclusions. Or as Jelaluddin Rumi says:

When you eventually see
through the veils to how things really are,
you will keep saying again
and again,
"This is certainly not like
we thought it was!"[3]

POSTURE

Regarding your posture during these and other practices, the key is
to arrange your body in a relaxed yet alert position, preferably with
your spine relatively vertical, so that it will not disturb you during
the practice period. Sitting cross-legged on a cushion or sitting in a
straight-backed chair is fine. Lying down or slumping in an easy
chair may be relaxing but it leads to drowsiness. The point is for
your body to help you stay present, clear, and undistracted.

THE PRACTICE OF SUBTLE OPENING

The practice of subtle opening has three parts:

1. YA LATIF

The practice begins with three to seven minutes of silent repetition
of the phrase *ya latif* (pronounced: ya la-TEEF) as a breathing prayer.
"*Ya*" means "oh" and signifies a calling forth of "*latif*" which means
"the most subtle, the most refined." Simply repeat the phrase silently
once on your in-breath and once on your out-breath.

Ya latif is an invocation of the subtlety of our being. By repeating
it we are invoking the essence of subtlety in us, its "felt sense." Explore this for yourself, opening ever more finely into the subtlety of
your being, and into the subtlety of the nature of being itself.

Latif is a special kind of word that tends to avoid becoming an
object. When we repeat it often enough, we may notice that it in-

deed invokes a felt sense of subtlety in our awareness — a lightness, an openness, an indefinably pure quality. This is because even though it is a noun, its "thingness" is not definite and does not offer an image to our imagination. What is signified by subtlety — when called forth in prayer like this — is not a substantial thing-in-itself but opens out to a quality beyond nouns or verbs or adjectives.

Another way of describing *latif-ness* is a sense of boundarylessness that you may experience as you invoke this breathing prayer. You might feel as if the edges of your body become slightly indefinable, or the back of your skull might feel as if it has disappeared. You might feel as if you are weightless or even invisible. These sensations are nothing to worry about; in fact, they are little graces on the path. Enjoy them!

Remember, this is a practice — we are practicing experiencing ourselves free from *here and there*, free from subject-object. Again, repeating *ya latif* is like practicing scales on a musical instrument — it is not the music itself, but it may help the music arrive.

2. The Four Signs

The second part of *the practice of subtle opening* is also a breathing prayer, repeated for three to seven minutes as well. Its intention is to help set you up for the recognition of timeless unconditioned awareness. But remember, expect nothing!

This breathing prayer consists of four words: *open, transparent, lucid,* and *awake.* Here there is a slight variation — only repeat these words on an in-breath. Let your out-breaths be silent, experiencing the invocation invoked. Therefore, simply repeat the word *open* silently on an in-breath, *transparent* on the following in-breath, *lucid* on the next in-breath, *awake* on the next in-breath, and then begin the cycle again.

These four words are "signs" that suggest (not define) aspects of pure contentless awareness. Like *ya latif,* they open out to qualities beyond their dictionary meanings. They are, by their very nature, subtle. As you repeat them, again let the felt sense of their meaning wash gently through you, one after the other. You don't have to struggle to sharpen that felt sense — it will accumulate by itself. Don't worry if sometimes you repeat a word and it fails to register a felt sense — it will the next time around, or the next. You will also discover that each sign modifies the others. By all means encourage this mutual modifying — there are mysteries here!

These four words describe qualities of this "no-thing" we are calling open awareness. Of course, this "no-thing" doesn't have qualities — so these four signs are at best suggestive. At worst, they will simply precipitate into concepts and there will be little benefit from their repetition.

Sincere engagement with this practice can lead to a sense of openness in our experience of existence. Initially this may be disorienting. I mentioned earlier the tenacity of subject-object dualism in our way of experiencing the world. As we invoke subtlety in our being through this practice, and the subtlety of recognizing open awareness — which is none other than recognizing our fundamental presence as *open, transparent, lucid,* and *awake* — we may be surprised to discover *the subject (self) doesn't exist as something particular and never did exist.*

In classical Sufi terms this recognition is called *fana,* or self-annihilation. But here we see that *fana* is not actually annihilation or ego-death, because no self ever existed that could undergo annihilation or death. There never was a subject! This is described succinctly by Ibn 'Arabi:

> You cannot know your Lord [This] by making yourself nothing. Many a wise man claims that in order to know one's Lord [This] one must denude oneself of the signs of one's existence, efface one's identity, finally rid oneself of one's self. This is a mistake. How could a thing that does not exist try to get rid of its existence? For none of matter exists. How could a thing

that is not, become nothing? A thing can only become nothing after it has been something. Therefore, if you know yourself without being, not trying to become nothing, you will know your Lord [This]. If you think that to know Allah [This] depends on your ridding yourself of yourself, then you are guilty of attributing partners to Him [the One] — the only unforgivable sin — because you are claiming that there is another existence besides Him [This], the All-Existent: that there is a you and a He [This].[4]

We will return to the principle of *fana* in future chapters — it is enough now to mention its potential in this present work and leave the experience to you.

Before we move on to the third part of *the practice of subtle opening,* let us look briefly at the "meanings" we might invoke as we repeat these four words: *open, transparent, lucid,* and *awake.*

Open

This sign points to the edgeless quality of nondual awareness. It is unconfined. Neither is there a center around which it condenses. It is open in all dimensions. Another way of interpreting the sign "open" is that it implies the infinite and all-pervading. The omnipresent. It suggests the sense that timeless awareness is not personal and is not confined to human beings or organic life-forms in general. The clear light of awareness is nonlocal. It is open. We may recognize it by this sign.

Transparent

This sign points to the quality of emptiness of nondual, primordial awareness. It is ontologically transparent. It is no thing, as in the Quran, 42,11: *No thing is like unto Him.* Unconditioned awareness, as well as our own nature and all existence, is open and transparent.

As the Buddha answered Shariputra when Shariputra asked him how one can awaken: *This most subtle awakening occurs through remaining at every moment attentive and attuned to the inherent openness and transparency of the various principles of manifestation, such as form and consciousness.* The transparent cannot be visualized. We may recognize it by this sign.

Lucid

This sign points to the quality of luminous clarity of open awareness. The word "lucid" means both utter clarity and radiance. Yet it is a light that is not the same as the light we see by in the outer world, as in the Quran, 24,35: *Light upon light!* This is lucidity that is transparent and without boundary. It is perfectly clear and cannot be stained. It is the "energy" that is the sustenance of being, of "amness." The Tibetans call it *Sambogakaya.* It is the energy that we experience as the very texture of existence. Like the transparent it cannot be visualized. It is the clear light. It cannot be hidden. We may recognize it by this sign.

Awake

This sign points to the quality of cognizant presence of boundless awareness. Being open, transparent, and lucid, awareness is naturally awake and present. Effort is not needed to make this be so. This awake quality is co-extensive with all existence and nonexistence, as in the Sufi prayer that speaks of the *omniscient, omnipresent, all-pervading, the Only Being.*[5] This sign is perhaps the most intimate and familiar of them all, since without trying we know the felt sense of *awake.* As the contemporary Buddhist teacher Tsoknyi Rinpoche writes, *Mind essence* [pure awareness] *is empty and originally so... When we actually experience it, what is it like? It's a feeling of being open, totally wide open...unconfined in any direction...not a concrete thing: not at all.... It is totally clear and wide awake, so there is nothing to pinpoint as "This is it."[6] It has neither back nor front: like space.* We may recognize it by this sign.

3. NON-DOING

The third part of *the practice of subtle opening* is both the easiest and the most subtle. Here we cease repeating all the breathing prayers and their subtle invocations and simply *sit doing nothing*. We "do" this for approximately five to ten minutes, or longer if time permits.

How do we do non-doing? By relaxing naturally, though remaining quiet and alert, and in an alert posture, as we have been for the previous parts of the practice. This is the Sufi teacher Inayat Khan's description of meditation: *mystical relaxation*. No effort. Even no effort at having no effort. We are simply still and present. What arises, arises. What passes, passes.

If we notice that we have become involved in what arises — thoughts or emotions — we don't bother about it, we simply notice it and allow it to pass without our further involvement. Non-doing is pure witness. We produce no interference with what occurs.

> *Since effort — which creates causes and effects, whether positive or negative — is unnecessary, immerse yourself in genuine being, resting naturally with nothing needing to be done. The expanse of spontaneous presence entails no deliberate effort, no acceptance or rejection. From now on make no effort, since phenomena already are what they are.*[7]
>
> —LONGCHENPA, FOURTEENTH-CENTURY
> DZOGCHEN MASTER

Many people have difficulty with *non-doing*. Even when we reduce our outward "doing" to an absolute minimum (sitting upright and still), inwardly the mind compensates by "doing" at a fierce rate. Since most of us are largely identified with our mind stream, this tends to make the practice of non-doing frustrating. *I can't stop doing my mind stream!*

In a future chapter we will turn to the subject of individual will and action implied in the word "doing." The question of the existence or nonexistence of free will can be disorienting in a useful way, but it can also produce a mass of thought constructions, which for our purposes at the moment would be distracting. For now we need to be concerned only with the practical questions that arise: ceasing all doing and acting for a period of five to ten minutes.

Here we might benefit from some advice of the great Hindu teacher Sri Nisargadatta Maharaj as he responds to a questioner who complains, "My thoughts won't let me rest."

> Pay no attention. Don't fight them. Just do nothing about them, let them be, whatever they are. Your very fighting them gives them life. Just disregard. Look through....You need not stop thinking. Just cease being interested. It is disinterestedness that liberates. Don't hold on, that is all. The world is made of rings. The hooks are all yours. Make straight your hooks and nothing can hold you. Give up your addictions. There is nothing else to give up. Stop your routine of acquisitiveness, your habit of looking for results, and the freedom of the universe is yours. Be effortless.[8]

· 3 ·

WHAT OBSCURES
OPEN AWARENESS?

Sometimes I am asked, "Why bother with all this? How will recognizing pure awareness benefit my life?" In response I am tempted to recite all the enticing benefits of recognition, including equanimity and inner peace, freedom, a sense of completion and ease, warmth in relationships, and a naturally arising happiness. Indeed, to become familiar with the spontaneous presence of pure awareness and to learn to open into its spaciousness *is* the "free medicine" the poets and mystics write about. The more time we spend resting in pure, contentless awareness, without interference, the more deeply we recognize it and the more naturally we gravitate back to its openness and ease. It is the fulfillment that is the goal of the spiritual quest.

But to speak of "benefits" is basically a detour, and to seek them is a dead end. Correctly speaking, there is no "goal" of the spiritual quest, since the lucid openness that is the ground of all being is already here. There is no "gravitating back to" because there is no separation. And there is no "quest" since there is nothing to look for. All of these ways of thinking obscure direct recognition. Direct recognition of open awareness does not result from thinking about it, or seeking it.

The spontaneous presence of open awareness is the very nature of here, now. We "arrive" by seeing there is nowhere to travel. Imagining that we have to go toward it is what creates the seeming distance. It is our natural state, and the natural state of all being. It is right in front of our eyes, and behind them too. Yet it is obviously difficult to recognize this natural state. What causes this difficulty? What obscures open awareness?

In this and future chapters we will consider some of the obstacles that seemingly hinder our recognition of pure and total awareness, and suggest methods and practices for releasing them. But in starting down this path, let us remind ourselves that methods and practices are not needed to produce or increase contentless awareness — it is completely and spontaneously present already. Methods and practices may be helpful only to the extent they serve to break loose habitual patterns of thinking and viewing ourselves and the world.

What obscures the recognition of open awareness is our deeply entrenched habit of attaching to, and identifying with, our thoughts and beliefs, the stories about reality that we tell ourselves — a process we are all intimately familiar with. This process operates on many levels, with its primary purpose being to create and maintain the illusion of a separate self — a self that must perpetually struggle to affirm its existence because it lives in the constant anxiety that it is fundamentally insubstantial. Releasing this sense of a personal, autonomous self — with its complexity of story-making, opinions, likes, dislikes, and anxieties — is an essential aspect of our work together.

However, as we have seen, the term "work" can be misleading, because it implies industriousness and effort. Perhaps we might more accurately call it non-work or non-doing, since the activity involved simply means opening to what we are naturally, prior to story-making or interpretations of any kind. It is a work as effortless as letting a child hold your hand.

IDENTITY MAKING

We create and maintain a sense of self, of personal reference point, in many ways. Here are a few of them:

- by restlessly doing one thing after another
- by assessing and separating our experience into likes and dislikes
- by asserting our imaginary power to decide about and control what happens in the future
- by craving things and experiences
- by continually interpreting the world around us and claiming we know it

These ways of living ever more powerfully reinforce the sense that I am a "subject" in relation to the "objects" of the world. "I" need to do this, and then that, and then that. "I" am the one who likes this and doesn't like that. "I" am captain of my destiny. "I" must have that. "I" know what is right and good. It isn't difficult to see how our sense of reality is gradually shaped by this process, and we become blinded by our false imaginings.

Many views attempt to describe the cause of our need to identify as a personal self and, as a consequence, separate ourselves so painfully from the world around us. Perhaps the most direct view in terms of our work together is simply to see that because our nature is fundamentally clear, open, and empty — that we are not, in fact, *entities* with any inherent self-ness — we are consequently subject to an existential anxiety of *groundlessness*. Our response to this anxiety is to try to fabricate a ground, some kind of identity that will convince us we are substantial and "real." As the nondual philosopher David Loy writes:

> ...our dissatisfaction with life derives from a repression even more immediate than death-terror: the suspicion that "I" am not real. The sense-of-self is not self-existing but a mental construction which experiences its groundlessness as a lack....We cope with this lack by objectifying it in various ways and try to resolve it through projects which cannot succeed because they do not address the fundamental issue....As long as we are driven by lack, every desire becomes a sticky attachment that tries to fill up a bottomless pit.[9]

Whatever the causes for creating a sense of a personal self out of nothing, the creation occurs, and its occurrence results in a kind of background noise that distracts us from recognizing our true nature. This noise expresses itself in the various obstacles to realization described in the following pages.

DOING

Perhaps the most constant obscuration of open awareness is *our compulsive need to do something next*. The desire to be distracted, to be stimulated, or to accomplish something succeeds in filling virtually every waking moment of our lives. This is such a constant habit that we barely notice it. From the moment we wake up in the morning until the moment we close our eyes at night we are *doing* something: daydreaming, strategizing, talking, moving, adjusting the comfort of our environment, or looking for ways to be entertained or distracted. As we have just seen, each of these forms of doing reinforces our position as a self in relation to the world "out there."

It is no wonder that as we first seek to recognize the clarity of our original nature, we ask what we can *do* to make this happen. Yet there is nothing we can do to recognize what we are — the recognition is prior to any doing on our part. We might think that *not-doing* in this way would be easy, but after a lifetime of practice we have become so identified with *being the doer* that not-doing is nearly synonymous with not-being. We might even say, "I do, therefore I am."

Of course, there are countless reasons for doing and staying busy. For one, we may be convinced that if we aren't preparing for what might be just around the corner, we will be caught off-guard and unprepared for what's coming. While preparing and planning obviously have an important role to play in our survival and in our creative relationship with society, we may use this natural function as a rationalization for perpetual busyness. Busyness increases to the level of a control-obsession, a belief that only by continuously doing or thinking can we adequately manipulate the future to suit our needs. Obsessive busyness in this way obscures our recognition of open awareness precisely because it is focused on achieving some future outcome, rather than allowing us to be open to what is. When we are open to what is, we are able to respond appropriately to what is needed in each situation without obsessing about it.

Another reason we may keep ourselves busy is to avoid the unpleasant feelings or sensations that may occur as we quiet down. Feelings of boredom, loneliness, sadness, or pain may arise as we settle into simple spontaneous presence. Constant activity may be our way of "cruising over" or repressing these undesirable feelings. Yet often it is only by experiencing our feelings with their full intensity in the moment that they yield their insight, release their hold on us, and resolve.

At the center of our need to always be doing something is dissatisfaction with the ways things are. Something could always be a little better — a little more intense, a little more relaxed, a little more stimulating, a little less overwhelming, a little warmer, a little cooler, a little more work, a little less work. We have a habit of thinking that "what is" is in constant need of adjustment.

This desire to change things is rooted in the wish to displace some present feeling. For example, the desire to eat something arises from the wish to displace a feeling of hunger or restlessness. The desire to have sex arises from the wish to displace the feeling of unexpressed arousal. The desire to shout angrily at someone arises from the wish to displace feelings of woundedness. When we recognize this dynamic and are able to observe it working in our stream of experience, we have the chance to relax our fixation on this need to displace a feeling, and in so doing we begin to free ourselves from acting impulsively. That "chance" is initially experienced as a little gap — a moment of seeing what is happening. As we practice noticing what is actually happening and thus giving more space around our thoughts, speech, and actions, this gap becomes larger and we simply observe without reactivity the internal phenomena of feelings and thoughts arising and then dissipating.

However, this doesn't mean we become dull or loveless or sit passively at home when we want to take a walk in the fresh air. We still act. In fact we act with more ease and spontaneity because we are not obsessed with trying to fulfill a mentally constructed reality. This is the difference between reactivity and acting spontaneously. Reactivity in this context means action that arises from the internal logic of our fixations. Spontaneous action is something altogether different.

As we learn to recognize our original nature and relax into its clear openness, we find there is no longer a need to generate a sense of self as the doer of actions. Action happens naturally, by itself. We do what comes to us to do. We are free to be present to this moment with whatever it has to offer.

One of the great nondual teachers of the twentieth century, Jean Klein, summarizes this theme of doing in the following way:

When you look deeply during doing, you'll see there is no room for an actor. There's only acting. It is only afterwards that the mind says, "I am doing it." Consciousness and its object are one. There cannot be doing and a feeling of being a doer at the same time. It may appear so but there is a very rapid movement from doing to doer. When you identify with the doer you will become tired. The fatigue is psychological. We all have had moments when we feel very tired but the moment something new or astonishing comes up that takes us away from ourselves, we are full of energy.[10]

LIKING AND DISLIKING

In future chapters we will look more extensively into the subject of preferring — of maintaining our sense of self by continually valuing or devaluing what appears in our awareness. Here we simply need to note how the dynamic of identity-making is fueled by our likes and dislikes, and particularly by our holding on to these preferences.

In one of the exercises suggested at the end of this chapter you will explore three types of listening: negative listening, positive listening, and pure listening. In this exercise you will get a profound, first-hand experience of how preferring what you hear — either positively or negatively — affects the quality of your encounter with others, as well as the quality of your sense of yourself. When you position yourself in judgment of others or of what is happening, that position reinforces your identification as a separate self. In this exercise you will also see that when you listen purely, without either validating or invalidating what is happening, you are simply open to what is. You are intimate with the world.

Here we can see how like/dislike reaction patterns have the potential to obscure our recognition of unconditioned awareness. Of course, attraction and aversion to phenomena are also essential aspects of our core survival responses — we avoid unpleasant sensations and are attracted to pleasant ones. However, there is an important difference between this kind of natural survival preference and the continual sorting of the world into good and bad, right and wrong, what I agree with and what I don't agree with. Preferring in this fashion is the common stuff of most social interactions and personal experience.

As long as we insist on judging what is occurring, we will not be able to be present with it. We will be caught in the net of our own position-taking. And the world will continue to disappoint us, since it often does not coincide with our preferences.

You can begin to explore this theme in your own life by watching how you react to things that you don't like, and how you attempt to assert what you do like. Once you begin to spot how this occurs in your daily experience — as with negative and positive listening — you can experiment with relaxing these positions of liking/disliking. At first you may still be flooded with signals that say, "I like this, I don't like this," or "I agree with this, I don't agree with this," or "this person is doing what I like, this person is doing what I don't like." Just let what happens happen, but don't react. Give space. Just be with what is occurring, including your preferences, but don't do anything about it.

Gradually the habit of sorting what happens in your experience into likes and dislikes will relax. You may still wish to express your view about something when it is appropriate, but the urgency will be gone. You will be free from the *need* to arrange the world according to your preferences.

The gift of this freedom is not only in reducing the stress of trying to get the world to agree with you. It more importantly frees you to open into your basic nature, the open awareness that is the backdrop of each moment, for this opening is no longer obscured by clinging to likes and dislikes, thoughts and position-taking.

WILLING AND CONTROLLING

One of the most stubborn mental patterns that obscures recognition of the spontaneous presence of pure awareness is generated by the illusion that "I" am an independent agent who can freely choose, decide, or will a thought or action. Simply put, volition obscures awareness. That is, the position I take when I consider myself the director of my actions and thoughts cannot help but create a sense of separation between this "position" and the world I believe I am manipulating. This sense of separation obscures recognition of the clear light of awareness.

Releasing our attachment to thinking of ourselves as independently willful beings is not easy. It is at the root of the idea of being a doer, and we are accustomed to arranging our view of reality and society according to the imperative that each one of us is responsible for his or her actions.

I encourage you to inquire directly into this assumption. Try to see how it is "you" make a choice. Look carefully at the very moment of a choice. Can you identify how you do it? Is there a little you inside your brain hemming and hawing about options, and then throwing a decision switch? What exactly happens when a choice is made?

For example, what determines the thoughts you think? Do you? If yes, how do you do that? If no, what does determine them? Or, another example, what determines the next movement you make? Look carefully. Try to see if there is someone — a you — choosing your next movement, and if so, can you see how that occurs?

The sense we have of conscious choice — free will — has recently been the subject of considerable scientific research. When volunteers were asked to note the moment they chose a specific movement and this process was simultaneously tracked with neurological scans, it was discovered that the feeling of conscious intention consistently *came after* brain signals had already initiated the movement. As one recent study concluded: "The feeling of the conscious intention to move does not cause movement genesis; both the feeling of intention and the movement itself are the result of unconscious processing."[11]

The point here is not to conclude that you have or don't have free will, but simply to allow for the possibility that your feeling that *you* are the controller of your actions may not be an accurate or complete description of how action occurs.

Here's another way to look at this: consider for a moment what is involved in our freedom to choose whether or not we stand up right now. Can we isolate that "choice" from the fact that we have feet to stand on, or the ability to balance ourselves, or the fact that someone built the floor on which we will stand, or that there is gravity, or that we were born, or that we are tired of sitting? Infinite conditions are implicated in every one of our "decisions." To claim that we have freedom of will in such an infinite context shrinks reality down to the size of our vanity.

You may also be able to appreciate here how the belief that I am an entity who can choose, decide, and control what happens puts me in a privileged position in relation to the rest of the universe. I take my place as a little god who can create something independently from whatever else may be happening. How wonderful! Now my fear of "groundlessness" can be overcome — I am indeed *something*: a decider, a chooser, a controller!

The nondual philosopher Wei Wu Wei, in his book *Why Lazarus Laughed*, offers these aphorisms regarding will and choice:

> Will is an imaginary function of an imaginary entity.

> As ultimate Reality we can have no will, for Non-Being [open awareness] is devoid of attributes.
>
> As relative Reality, in the dualistic aspect of Consciousness and objects of Consciousness, Observer and all that is observed, we are integrated in the Cosmos and act accordingly.

As individuals we are merely figments and cannot have will other than as desire and its opposite.

Will, therefore, is just a figure of speech.

We are like passengers in a railway train who think that we can change our mind and make the train go anywhere we wish.[12]

In terms of cultivating the conditions within which we may recognize open awareness and sustain the realization of its spontaneous presence, it is essential that we look sincerely for actual evidence that our individual will is the original cause of our actions. I have suggested several ways (above, and in the exercises at the end of this chapter) for you to explore this question on your own. I am not interested in convincing you one way or another about this age-old issue, nor is it important that you arrive at a definite conclusion about it. What is important is your direct encounter with the question, free of assumptions. Live this question!

KNOWING AND MAKING MEANING

Let us consider now the functions of "knowing" and "making meaning" as they, too, obscure recognition of the spontaneous presence of clear awareness. Each of us has been well schooled in the benefits of being knowledgeable and constructing meaning out of experiences. Having conceptual knowledge is associated with intelligence, success, control, psychological skill, and security. The more elaborate our story about who we are, what we stand for and what is going on, the more secure we feel. While there is of course nothing wrong with this kind of knowing, and it can certainly be of great value, it can also be its own kind of prison. "This was a good day, yesterday was a bad day" is a modest example of making meaning. "I have never been successful and this is because my father didn't acknowledge me" is another more psychological kind of knowing.

We create a story about almost everything and then we live inside it. We forget that we are not compelled to make everything meaningful. It is possible to just be with what is without needing to understand it, interpret it, or make it significant.

In learning to recognize and rest in open awareness, the need to make meaning and interpret what is happening can work against us. When we are attached to knowing we are continually scanning our experience for definitions, analogies, comparisons, and other ideas that will orient us. The very activity of knowing in this way relies upon a subject-object dichotomy — which, to repeat, is often useful in everyday life. However, in opening our experience to the reality of our original nature, the subject-object point of reference is an obstacle to our realization. It obscures the Real with the wallpaper of our opinions, and the point of reference remains the insistent "I," "me," and "mine."

This is where it is helpful to relax into what mystics call "not-knowing" or "un-knowing." At the conditioned level, not-knowing means not judging, not asserting, and not painting the path in front of ourselves with our own preconceptions and opinions. From the perspective of unconditioned awareness, not-knowing means there is nothing to know, nothing to work out, nothing to analyze. We cannot understand the unconditioned experience because there is absolutely nothing finite to understand. (Yet everything we do know remains immediately accessible. Unconditioned awareness is not a trance state.)

> *Knowings of the veil*
> *cannot bear what appears*
> *when the veil is torn.*[13]
>
> —NIFFARI, TENTH-CENTURY SUFI

How do we relax into not-knowing? One way is through prayer, and the humility that is prayer's natural context. Also meditation, with its practice of witnessing without interference, can train us to notice how thoughts and sensations arise and dissolve on their own, loosening our sense of their importance and our attachment to them. Still another way is through moment-by-moment vigilance of our assumptions and opinions in daily life. Our process of self-inquiry can include questions such as, *Do I really know that? Is this view of mine part of a larger story that I keep telling myself? What is actually my experience now?* Questions such as these reduce our certainty and open the possibility of catching the "I" in the process of solidifying itself.

When first engaging in the process of opening to the spontaneous presence of unconditioned awareness, it is common for people to construct beliefs and ideas about what unconditioned awareness is and what it means. This may occur in reaction to the teaching that open, contentless awareness is "nothing" and has no "meaning." These radical statements can sound cold or abstract, and invite the addition of qualifiers and attributes, such as "divine" or "sacred," or more complex religious narratives. At first glance, it is indeed disconcerting to consider that the Real does not present any graspable story or thinkable doctrine, or that it cannot be an object of understanding.

For many spiritual seekers this formlessness can be especially challenging. We may have spent decades developing beliefs and ideas about practice or the meaning of life, the qualities of the divine or the difficulty of the mystical path. Even the idea that we are on the right path points to a belief system about right and wrong paths. Likewise we can become consumed by our search for freedom or driven by the need to deliver others from their ignorance and suffering. All of these ideas are constructions (whether they are held personally or collectively) and limit our actual experience of the unimpeded, indefinable awareness that is what Sufis call *wadat al-wajud* — the Oneness of Being.

We can never interpret or "know" the Oneness of Being. It is unconditioned and thus has no structures or limits, no center and no edge. There is no place from which it came and no place to which it goes. We might say it is nothing, and yet it is beyond being nothing or something. In fact, even to give it names like we do: *pure awareness, self-existing unconditioned awareness, our original nature, openness, etc.,* risks placing it into some kind of metaphysical category. Self-existing awareness or openness doesn't actually exist — at least in the way we usually think of existence. As signifiers, these names and what they signify are "permanently under erasure, deployed for tactical reasons but denied any semantic or conceptual stability." (Loy) Nevertheless, what we are talking about is present throughout; it is all-pervasive. It simply cannot be known as we know the phenomenal things of the world.

As I mentioned earlier, it is initially helpful to be able to distinguish between conditioned experience and unconditioned awareness. Otherwise we may think we are experiencing unconditioned awareness when in fact we are experiencing a lightly structured state of mind and heart in which we are still identified with certain spiritual thoughts or feelings. For example, thinking we know what is happening or enjoying a spiritual feeling can still be an obstacle created by our interpretations of reality.

This is a subtle and important point. It is not to say anything is wrong with having spiritual ideas, feelings, or beliefs, but simply that we need to recognize these for what they are: constructions of our conditioned thinking, which may or may not be helpful to begin orienting us on the path. However, they are not, and cannot be, the destination itself, which is beyond all ideas and feelings. Clinging to specific interpretations of reality limits our experience of what is beyond the reach of our conceptions and beliefs.

FEAR OF VANISHING

Another set of beliefs and projections that can occur early in this work are conscious and unconscious fears about death or loss of control. For example, some people may think that by opening to the spontaneous presence of open awareness they will lose touch with the real world and become less capable of fulfilling their daily commitments. If they give up their attachments to liking and disliking, approving or disapproving, and just "accept what is," life will become bland, boring and uninteresting. Or worse yet, they will not do anything at all and simply become passive. Others may think that because pure awareness is described as being empty of structure and content, it must resemble a barren, unfeeling, and lifeless blank field. Clearly, if we have these projections we will develop an aversion to the experience.

In part, these fears may arise from the initial sense of disorientation that can be experienced when hearing about or first opening to the possibility of awareness that is contentless. If "it" is empty or nothing, then what am I? Where am I? Is this nihilism?

There may be a sense that somehow what is at stake is the whole ego project itself. "I" am real as long as I desire or reject things, or as long as I like, dislike, or am bored by things. If I were to stop liking or disliking, who would I be? Would I vanish? Opening to the spontaneous presence of pure awareness is in fact a primal challenge to the ego's sense of existence, so it is no wonder that fears of groundlessness and loss of identity would arise.

At this level the work requires great courage. How do we not run from this seeming effacement of our existence? Throughout history, mystics have been able to pass this threshold by having cultivated deep faith, either in a religious narrative or as a sense of trust in the personal guidance and blessing of a revered teacher. This trusting capacity, combined with the release of one's need to know, provides the basis of relaxation by which one may let go of the idea of oneself and recognize what is already true:

> Certainly you are not you; yet you do not know. Know that
> this existence is neither you nor not you. You do not exist; yet

you are also not a nonexistence…Without being and without
not-being, your existence and your nonexistence is Allah's
being, because it is certain that the being of the truth is the
same as your being and your not-being, and at the same time
the truth is you and not-you.[14]

—IBN AL'ARABI

As we read these kinds of statements from the point of view of
our conditioned experience, we may feel an uncomfortable confusion. If we don't give up at this point, this kind of confusion can become an ally. It gives us a hint how deeply the work of nondual
awakening is proceeding, and helps to dislodge the fixity of our self-
concept.

NOTHING OBSCURES OPEN AWARENESS

Up to now, this chapter has focused on various ways in which recognition of the spontaneous presence of unconditioned awareness may
be obscured. Yet even the very idea that this can happen — that open
awareness can be obscured — can be misleading, and can itself obscure our recognition.

As we are beginning to appreciate, open awareness — the ever-
present, timeless ground of being that is our most intimate nature —
is not something that something else can get in the way of. Deter-
mining what obscures open awareness is simply a way of thinking
and speaking, a pedagogical style that may be provisionally useful
but is basically a concept and nothing more.

The ground of being has no form. There is nothing to obscure.
Our conditioned experience, i.e., our need to do, to know, to make
meaning, etc., cannot "get in front of" spontaneous presence.

So what are we doing here? We are simply opening into the nature
of paradoxes without trying to resolve their seeming contradictions.

We are beginning to recognize that action occurs without a doer or a chooser. We are beginning to recognize we no longer need to make an identity by asserting our preferences to others and ourselves. We are beginning to recognize that our well-practiced abilities to "know" things and to construct interpretations about what is real are limited tools, useful in many practical situations but not helpful for recognizing the Oneness of Being.

Indeed, "recognizing" the Oneness of Being does not occur in the same way we recognize this sentence or its meaning, or anything else that is phenomenal. While this may be confusing at this point, we are beginning to allow the possibility that there could be another way of recognition that does not involve a subject "recognizing" an object. It is a recognition that occurs through *being recognition*. It is the end of witnessing, of being separate from what is known. Recognition in this regard happens all at once, without dependence on memory or interpretation.

In this way we begin to recognize that nothing can obscure the spontaneous presence of open awareness, because nothing can get in-between our being and Being.

Exercises: What Obscures Open Awareness?

1. Personal Inventory

Give yourself time to write answers to the following questions. Your answers don't have to be in full sentences — short phrases or even lists of words are fine — but engage with the introspection sincerely.

RESTLESSNESS

1   What kind of situations make you feel restless?
2   What kind of physical sensations accompany your restlessness?
3   Do you have typical "stories" or interpretations that arise concerning these feelings of restlessness, like explaining to yourself that these sensations are bad or good, or they mean this or that, or they will lead to worse feelings, etc.?
4   What do you do to remove or reduce these sensations?

BOREDOM

1   When do you feel bored?
2   What is your experience with meditation (all kinds) and boredom?
3   What does it feel like when you are bored? Try to describe this feeling.
4   What do you typically do to remove or reduce this feeling?

STIMULATION

1 Describe your typical routines for keeping your mind active.

2 What kinds of activities do you turn to when you want to be "distracted?" (TV, books, shopping, etc.)?

3 When you turn to activities that offer distraction, what are the feelings that occur just before you turn?

4 What do you most often want to be distracted from?

MAKING MEANING

1 Some of the ways we make meaning are by constructing and maintaining stories about who we are and what we stand for. Try to describe a few of the common stories you use when explaining to people who you are and what you stand for.

2 In a similar way, describe in summary form a few of the common stories you tell others about your psychological make-up — why you have such-and-such a pattern, what events in your early life caused you to be such-and-such a way, etc.

3 List three things that you know to be true, and then describe how you know them to be true.

2. Noticing Behavior Patterns

Over the course of the next two to three weeks, notice the following behavior patterns in your daily life. There is no need to try to change these behaviors or judge yourself for having them, simply notice their occurrence. Of course, you may find you forget to notice these patterns for part or all of a day. That's okay, just notice them as often as you can.

1 Notice your need to be doing something next.

2 Notice when you seem to be making a problem out of a problem, that is, when you magnify some issue that needs to be attended to with anxiety, distress, judgments, etc.

3   Notice when you start to create "stories," i.e., reviewing
    and making interpretations, corrections, elaborations,
    conclusions, etc., about what is happening or has hap-
    pened.
4   Notice when you sort your experience into what you like
    and what you don't like, what you approve of and what
    you don't approve of.

3. Positive, Negative, and Pure Listening

This exercise is best done with a friend in a staged, role-playing way.
It takes about ten minutes, and is well worth the time. If you can't
find a partner to do this with, you can explore it in your own way
whenever you are listening to someone. You can also observe these
styles of listening in others, especially positive and negative listening.
(*I am grateful to Peter Fenner and Marie Barincou for inspiring this
exercise.*)

1. Positive Listening

Ask your friend to start talking about something — an issue in their
life, a memory from the past, an opinion, whatever. Silently listen
to them in a positive way, with interest in what they are saying. Don't
speak, but you can validate what they are saying by nonverbally giving energy to their story and encouraging them to continue. You
will be very familiar with this type of listening. Feel free to give little
cues to your friend, both with sounds and in your body language,
that show you are interested and affirm what they are saying, although refrain from turning this into a conversation. This is an exercise in listening. Notice how this style of positive listening seems
to affect what your friend is saying and how they feel. Do this and
the next two styles of listening for about three to four minutes each.

2. Negative Listening

With your friend continuing to talk, now silently listen to them in a negative way, with no real interest in what they are saying but with a minimum of politeness so you don't just get up and walk away. In negative listening, you have no interest in validating what your friend is saying, and you wish they would stop talking. You experience yourself disconnected and detached, and involved in your own thoughts. Notice how this style of negative listening seems to affect what your friend is saying and how they feel.

3. Pure Listening

With your friend continuing to talk, now silently listen to them in neither a positive way nor a negative way. Simply listen with full attention to what they are saying, but without any investment on your part that they either continue to talk or stop talking. You neither validate what they are saying nor invalidate it. You are fully present, but you have no judgment or agenda of your own. If you experience yourself interpreting or assessing what they are saying, listen to that in the same way you are listening to their talk — without a bias of any kind. Notice how this style of pure listening seems to affect what your friend is saying and how they feel.

Take a few moments with your friend after this exercise to check how it was for them while you listened in these three ways.

4. Willing, Choosing, and Controlling

Here are several suggestions for exploring the question of individual will. Explore them slowly, with curiosity. Be the scientist of your own experience.

1   Intentionally generate a thought about something, or an image of something. As you do this, look carefully to see how you do it. How did you choose that thought? Why? Try this again. See if you can find how, and if, the intention to gener-

ate that thought or image actually does so. Is there a connection between the thought or image that appears and the intention to have it?

2   Think about an issue in your life. As you do so, see if you can discover how you think. Do you *will* what you think? If so, that means you are in control of this thinking process. How do you do that?

3   Try to remember the names of each of your elementary school teachers. Watch, as you try this, how you do it and how you are in control of the process.

4   Sit with your hands resting on your thighs. Looking carefully at the moment of choice, lift your right hand when you choose to do so. Can you find what it is that makes that choice?

5   Make a movement you want to make. Now make a movement you don't want to make. Is it possible to do the latter?

6   Now again make a movement that you want to make. See if you can find out where the "want to" comes from. Do you control that?

· 4 ·

NOTICING MENTAL CONSTRUCTIONS AND FIXATIONS

Next we must undertake the observation of our desires so as to understand what it is that we are really seeking... What is desired is bliss, Ananda, which exists at all times in myself and in everything. The realization of the presence of this bliss was lost to me when I became a separate ego, thereby losing sight of my essential identity with it. From that moment on, the world of objects and duality was born. This duality makes it impossible for us to perceive the presence of this bliss which abides in ourselves as in all things.[15]

—JEAN KLEIN

In the previous chapter and exercises we explored some of the ways in which the spontaneous presence of open awareness can be obscured. We identified several patterns of thinking, feeling, and behaving that keep us identified with our conditioned existence. We focused especially on the ways in which we produce a sense of identity or personal selfhood: by identifying as *the doer* of our actions, as the one who maintains a field of *likes and dislikes*, as the one who *wills* what he or she does, and as the one who *makes meaning* out of what happens. We also considered the subtext of all these strategies for producing an identity: the fear of vanishing, of being nothing.

The points summarized in the preceding paragraph can bring up a host of objections — for example: Of course I am the "doer" of my actions, who else could be? Of course I have "likes and dislikes," how else can I negotiate my way in life, or enjoy things? Of course I will what I do, how else can my obvious freedom to choose be explained? Of course I make meaning out of what happens, how else could I know right from wrong, or care about anything?

These kinds of objections frequently occur when one is first confronted with the paradoxes of nondual awareness. Notice in each case the prominence of the idea of the "I" and its self-appointed roles. By its own logic, the "I" insists that it is what keeps everything happening. But if we look carefully at *what* is happening and *how* it happens, we see an infinite field of causes and conditions implicated in the least action — the blinking of your eye for example, or the falling of a single raindrop. When we consider that the existence of the entire universe is implicated in this ever-flowing, spontaneous moment, then we see there is never just a single cause or a single agent for an action. Your capacity to read this sentence, and the fact that you are doing so right now, is not the result of "your" choice to do so. It is an action that is, in effect, causeless, since we cannot identify any one cause or series of causes that makes it possible. For us to think there is an "I" that can choose or act independently from the rest of reality is the very fantasy that creates the conditions for feelings of alienation and existential loneliness. (The subject of causality, and whether or not there really is a dynamic of "cause" and "effect" in an ultimate, nondual sense, goes beyond our purposes here. Suffice it to say that your reading this sentence may very well be causeless because the infinite spontaneity of all being, of which your reading this sentence is a part, is fundamentally causeless.)

Nevertheless, the notion that there is an "I" is a durable one. As we have seen, the "I" continually produces stories about reality, maintaining its illusion of existence through the leading role it plays in all of them. In this chapter we will explore some of the typical ways in which we construct stories about who we are and what is real. We will see how we become attached to these stories, thus making *fixations* out of them, and we will consider the root cause of this process: the tendency to divide our experience into what we like and what we dislike.

Once we become more adept at noticing the patterns of our likes and dislikes, and the mental constructions and fixations that we assemble around them, we can begin to unhook from the reactivity such patterns engender. In this way we become free to live more natural and spontaneous lives. And beyond this gift, we become ever more available to recognize unconditioned open awareness as the ground of our being, and of all being.

LEARNING TO NOTICE MENTAL CONSTRUCTIONS AND FIXATIONS

Mental constructions are simply the stories we constantly tell ourselves about the meaning of our experience. They are how we interpret reality, what we believe to be true, our judgments and opinions. Rather than being descriptive or faithful to what is, they often create layers of additional interpretations that distort our experience of reality. If we become *attached* to these stories, they become what we call fixations.

For example, let's imagine that coming home from work after a hard day, I stumble on the front step while carrying in the groceries.

Now I might just pick up myself and the groceries and continue inside, constructing nothing out of the incident. However, I might instead feel a flash of anger. Already I have started constructing something, even on this nearly unconscious level: *somebody must be at fault for this.* I look around for the causes of my anger. *Who distracted me? Who didn't fix the step? Why do I always have to do the shopping?* In a relatively short time these causes or conditions for my situation are painted with an increasingly elaborate story in my mind. Soon, long histories and multiple people and future predictions are all woven into a reinforcing belief: *I do everything around here. No one notices how overworked I am. They never did care for me as much as they do for themselves. I need a new house.* While I might have been free in the beginning to notice the anger and let it relax in its own time, I now have such a sequence of ideas, beliefs, and feelings that the whole experience feels solid, dense, and unalterable. The construction is becoming a fixation. Of course, sometimes constructions simply arise and then dissipate — temporary little complaints about the world. But at other times they reinforce the constellation of fixations we have built throughout our life, and become part of them.

As we see with this example, constructions — and the fixations that arise from them — often develop around simple problems. Things don't go the way we want them to. We experience a problem. Then we begin to add layers of interpretation. We make more problems out of our problem. Recognizing how and when we construct these stories or problems is essential in releasing our belief in their truth, and opening into spontaneous presence.

Whenever we suspect we are creating a storyline, we can ask ourselves simple questions like: Is there something being constructed here? What am I doing now? Am I making a problem out of a problem? Am I making up a story? What is the story really about? What is the root feeling that is being elaborated here?

It's also helpful to recognize the surface signs of constructions and fixations as they are being manufactured. When we experience ourselves expressing inwardly or outwardly any of the following signs, there is a strong likelihood that we are constructing a story, or are already under the sway of a fixation (or a cluster of them):

- self-defense, self-protection
- justifications, rationalizations, excuses
- complaints
- anger
- self-pity
- blames: self-directed or other-directed
- categorical statements
- repeating something you say often
- talking at length about yourself or others
- having strong opinions
- insisting on something

You might think of other symptoms too. We can see from this list that each behavior mentioned implies *identification with a story or point of view*. Since each of us attaches to very different stories and points of view over the course of a lifetime, we can see there is nothing absolute about any of our stories — they are merely the result of a particular stream of conditions at the moment and do not reflect "the truth," whatever that might be. The opinions, defensiveness, complaints, and judgments, etc., that we felt a year ago, or five years ago, are simply no longer relevant. They don't reflect "the truth" now. In fact, they never did.

When we can clearly see how our blaming, complaining, worrying, justifying, and insisting have no reliable basis, we can finally relax. We can stop, right in the middle of a sentence or an argument or a worried thought stream. Since it takes effort to produce the story or maintain a point of view, stopping actually requires nothing. We just relax.

Learning to catch ourselves mid-stream and relax from our effort of constructing stories in this way is a rare skill of character, and is a gift for others to witness. We don't need to get too serious about this process; when you think about it, the most delightful people to be around are those with a nonjudgmental and humorous view of themselves.

FIXATIONS AND THEIR ROOTS

Ultimately, living our lives under the delusion of fixations drains our energy and spirit. The Australian Buddhist nondual teacher Peter Fenner in his ground-breaking work *Radiant Mind*, gives a succinct description of fixations as the source of our suffering:

> Whereas early Buddhist texts identify the source of suffering as craving or grasping, the Middle Path, or Madhyamaka, tradition of Buddhism uses the term "fixation." The actual Sanskrit word is *drshti*, meaning "fixed opinion or belief," but I prefer the term "fixation" because it bridges the psychological, cognitive, and energetic aspects of the phenomenon.
>
> Fixation refers to the way we grasp onto ourselves and the things that make up our world, believing these to be either real or illusory. Fixation occurs whenever we take a rigid and inflexible position about any aspect of our experience. When we're fixated, we invest mental, emotional, and physical energy in focusing on one particular interpretation of reality....
>
> When we're fixated, we see things through dualistic categories, such as good or bad, right and wrong, self and other, one and many. We're either happy or miserable, free to do what we want or controlled by our circumstances, responsible

or not responsible for our behavior. We're progressing toward our goal, or we aren't. People are either enlightened or unenlightened. To the extent we're fixated, we introduce a bias or distortion into our experience of ourselves and the world.... Rather than seeing things as they are, we view the world through the filter of our opinions and preferences, likes and dislikes, and we're constantly trying to avoid what we don't like and to obtain or prolong what we do.[16]

As Fenner points out, the root cause of fixations can be traced back to our identification with our likes and dislikes. We tend to react to our experience in one of two ways — either: (1) I like this, I approve of it, I want more of it; or (2) I don't like this, I don't approve of it, I want it to stop.

Of course, on one level this is quite natural — as organic beings we seek to sustain life through this fundamental preferring. We build shelter to protect us from the rain and snow, we find food when we are hungry, we withdraw our hand when it touches a candle flame.

But as complex human beings embedded in a complex civilization, this natural, survival-based preferring has extended to situations far beyond survival needs. Our patterns of attraction and aversion have become highly elaborate structures through which we identify ourselves. In fact, identification, attachment, attraction, aversion — these are different ways to speak about the same process responsible for forming the illusion of a personal, separate self. The "I" believes it has found evidence for its existence because "I" am the one who likes this or dislikes that. "I am my likes and dislikes."

As we settle ever more deeply into the web of our preferences, we spin more webs to rationalize or judge what is happening around us. We say, *This is good; this is bad. I approve of this; I don't approve of that.* For example, here is a typical preference stream: *I don't want those people to come over tonight. I don't feel good. Anyway, I don't look good today. My hair's a mess. It must be that new shampoo. I never wanted to buy it anyway. It was that clerk in the pharmacy who talked me into it.* Etc. We construct an internal logic to rationalize our preferences, and the result is our being convinced of its efficacy. We become insistent.

Insistency is a hallmark of fixations. We lose our capacity for equanimity and flexibility, and instead align our wellbeing with the demand that things turn out just as we want them. Or in situations when we confront something we don't like — for example, the statement of a politician we don't approve of — we react with a torrent of judgment and insistent righteousness.

We may be tempted to think that fixations are obviously unreasonable reactions and we, being more reasonable beings, are not susceptible to them. But this is not the case. The subtle and not-so-subtle presence of our likes and dislikes is with us wherever we go. We react positively or negatively to this noise or that voice, this idea or that feeling. For many people this "fixation reaction" is so deeply ingrained it becomes the primary way they encounter reality: sorting it according to what is acceptable and what is not, what they want to continue and what they want to stop.

Another way to look at the root cause of fixations is to see that identifying with our likes and dislikes is an expression of *need*. By aligning my identity with things I like and things I don't like, I am implicitly defining myself as incomplete. That is, I *need* my world to produce things I like and to protect me from things I don't like. When this strategy is successful, when the world does produce things I like, then I *need* it to keep doing that. When the world produces things I don't like, I *need* it to change. Thus the "I," as a being defined by its likes and dislikes, is by definition a being in need. Something is always missing for the I. This perpetual insecurity is the I's defining characteristic. The I can never be complete or whole, though it tries to manufacture wholeness by possessing things, people, sensations, or mental conclusions in the form of opinions and beliefs.

As we shall see as we proceed in this work, releasing the primal fixation of needing things to be different allows the possibility of opening into the spontaneous presence of self-occurring awareness. When the formation of the needy "I" is seen for what it is — simply an idea and not a fact — we are able to let it go. We are able to let things be just as they are. Letting things be allows us to accept what life presents without interfering with it through our neediness or our contriving to make things different. We accept what is because it is. We are wide open. From the spaciousness of our openness we are free to respond spontaneously and without the turbulence created by needing things to be different.

It is important to note that the emphasis here is on *attachment to outcome*. This is the root quality of the tendency to divide our experience into what we like and what we don't like. We are of course still able to enjoy a hot shower more than a cold one, or a kiss more than a look of disdain. But if the hot water runs out, or someone judges us, we don't need to make a big deal out of it. It simply is what is. We don't need to load the situation with attachment to our liking things to be a certain way. What occurs, occurs. We rest *in* clear awareness and *as* clear awareness — no matter what occurs. Then we don't contribute our suffering or resistance to the situation.

We will return to this point shortly, because there is more to explore regarding how we act without preferring, but first let's consider some of the dynamics of observing and releasing fixations.

NOTICING FIXATIONS

Before we can free ourselves from fixations and their reactivity, we must *learn to notice them*. We begin by simply observing what is happening, by noticing the patterns of our preferences, our likes and dislikes. Notice the shape and recurrence of your feelings of neediness. It is not necessary to analyze why you have these preferences;

simply notice that you do. Notice how your sense of identity is woven into this pattern of attractions and aversions.

But don't become obsessed with fixing your fixations — that's another kind of insistence. Just see them for what they are. It is helpful to be a bit lighthearted about this. Many people report that at a certain point they begin to see fixations everywhere. They are dismayed and disappointed with themselves, or with others whose fixations are also on display. This is where lightheartedness and compassion are helpful. Remember, fixations do not actually exist as something solid or immovable. They are patterns of thought and reactivity. They vanish when not repeated.

I highly recommend this practice of noticing your preferences and attraction-aversion tendencies. While it isn't always comfortable, it will serve you well. As you learn to notice your basic responses in terms of liking or disliking what's happening to you or around you, the attachments you have to these responses will, on their own, loosen their grip.

One reason for this loosening is because learning to notice your patterns of preferring involves a shift from identifying as the person defined by those preferences to simply being a neutral observer. Sometimes this neutral space of observation is called "creating the witness." The idea of being a witness allows the creation of some space around your likes and dislikes, which may have been experienced up to this time as an essential part of your identity. If the idea of being a witness is helpful for you, by all means use it. Just realize that the notion of the witness is an intermediate step. There really is no witness as such. There is witnessing — awareness itself — but no entity that witnesses.

Below are a number of situations we all encounter in life. They represent typical circumstances in which our identification with our likes and dislikes is fairly apparent. Observe yourself closely as you encounter them in your daily life. What do you notice about yourself and your reactive tendencies of liking something or disliking it?

- Notice when you are trying to justify yourself. Notice how you feel at those times and what you want to happen, or not happen.
- Notice when you feel embarrassment or uncertainty about your appearance or something you say. Conversely, notice when you feel pride about these things. Notice how you act or what you start thinking about when you feel either embarrassment or pride in these ways. See if you can notice what you want to happen or not happen in these situations.
- Notice when you try to draw attention to yourself, like talking loudly, interrupting others, or trying to make others laugh. What prompts this? What do you want to happen, or not happen?
- Notice when you try to avoid having attention turned to you, like when you avoid contact or conversation. What prompts this? What do you want to happen, or not happen?
- Notice when you try to please people. Notice the particular ways you do this — through words and actions. What do you want to happen?
- Notice when you resist other people and what they say or want. Notice the particular ways you do this, how you are critical, judgmental, or attempt to blame or correct people. What do you want to avoid happening?
- Notice when you are critical or judgmental about yourself. See if you can notice how you think this criticism is true. What is the evidence? Is it permanently true or provisionally true?
- Notice when you try to intensify your experience — through substances, bodily exertion, talk, or "mental catastrophizing."

What do you want to happen, or not happen? Notice the root sensation in these instances when you are feeling you don't want the present state to continue, when you want to intensify your experience. Observe that preference, how it arises in your awareness and how you make constructions and fixations around it, and then identify with them.

- Notice when you disagree strongly with what others are saying or doing, or when you become angry. Notice the quickness of your reaction to them. What is happening there? What is the preference that motivates your reaction?

These situations are examples; you may discover many others as you make this practice your own. As it evolves, you will notice a gradual opening of your experience. There will begin to occur more space around your reactions to what others say or do, or around your own assertiveness or reluctance. The point is not to engage in a lengthy analysis of your desires and their causes, simply to notice your preference that something continue or stop.

ACTING WITHOUT BIAS

Learning to live and act free from the bias of our likes and dislikes is a subject that often produces confusion or argument. Sometimes people object to this approach by using examples related to survival situations: for example, *the house is on fire — do I accept what is and just sit there?* Of course not. The same is true for responding to injustice. Resting in the spontaneous presence of open awareness doesn't mean we are passive. By being fully present to what is we can respond more appropriately when a response is called for. We do what is obvious. We just don't waste our energy or the energy in a situation with turbulent reactions stemming from our fixations and the needy identification that underlies them.

Other objections to living and acting without bias include questions like the following: Are you saying that desire and preferences are wrong? How else do I make decisions or make things happen or stop them from happening? It's natural to feel passion or anger or embarrassment! Are you saying that I should resist these natural feelings?

As I mentioned above, the emphasis here is on *attachment to outcome*, not on the simple inclination to either experience or not experience something. When I use the words *liking, disliking, desiring,* and *preferring,* I am pointing to the grasping quality of these experiences. As with many areas in the discourse of nonduality, there do not seem to be adequate words to describe, for example, desire that does not grasp. Perhaps we could call it inclination, or openness, or natural responsiveness.

If, for example, you stop on a path to smell a rose and bend down toward it, that movement could be called natural responsiveness. Now if someone calls to you at just that moment, causing you to turn your head and stand up, thus missing the moment of smelling the rose, you could either be annoyed because you were interrupted, or be completely present to the person who called to you. The difference in these two reactions is the difference caused by attachment or its absence. (And we could also stand this example on its head: you are about to smell the rose and then hear someone calling your name, but you intuitively know this person is just trying to draw attention to himself. In this case, you have no attachment to social politeness either, and continue smelling the rose.)

What we are inviting here is the possibility of living free from bias and attachments, without needing things to be a certain way — *simply accepting what is while still being completely responsive to whatever shows up in the moment.*

As we learn to open to nondual awareness, we begin to notice the vast field of our preferences and the thoughts, feelings, and actions that arise from those preferences. We just notice. Gradually our noticing them begins to reduce their insistence and reactivity. We experience more space around our thoughts, feelings, and actions. That spaciousness begins to be experienced as a greater and greater sense of equanimity. Serenity opens in our life. We no longer lead with our likes, dislikes, and opinions. We simply are present to what is. No clamoring for it, and no avoidance or denial of it. We accept what is simply because it is, including our feelings about it. We are no longer a victim of those feelings, or of the root preferences they grow from. Likes, dislikes, feelings, identifications, attachments — these may arise, but we don't experience ourselves as stuck to them. They are simply objects and sensations in our awareness. They arise and vanish, as do all objects and sensations in our awareness.

RELEASE AT INCEPTION

In a future chapter we will explore the dynamic described by the fourteenth-century Tibetan Dzogchen master Longchenpa, called *release at inception.* I would like to introduce it here briefly, however, as a way to conclude this chapter. My hope is it will serve to ease any possible sense you may have, after reading all of this, that mental constructions and fixations represent problems requiring a lot of skill and effort to get rid of. They don't. Yes, fixations have a stubborn tendency to show up again and again in our mind stream — that's why they're called fixations — but in themselves they are like all other mental phenomena that arise in our awareness: they originate out of nothing (that is, they aren't there before they are), seem to abide for a moment or two (although they don't exactly "abide" in a fixed way), and then they vanish back into nothing without any effort on our part. They are released naturally.

You can test this for yourself right now. Try to generate the feeling-tone of one of your common fixations — for example, a typical situation in which you feel you need to justify yourself. If you are successful at generating this feeling-tone, even to a small degree, you may notice that the pattern of the fixation, with its accompanying emotional state, arises in your awareness for a moment or two, and then begins to dissipate, and will vanish altogether unless you repeat the thought or image that stimulated it.

Over the next twenty-four hours you might try this again with a few real-life "fixation situations." For example, there may be a situation in which you feel unsure of yourself and don't know what to do. Notice that the thought-feeling of uncertainty appears, seems to abide for a while, and then naturally dissolves into the next thing that happens. And if you look carefully you may notice that even in the moments when it seems to "abide," it is changing and moving, becoming stronger, diminishing, adding new elements, etc. It doesn't even "abide" as the same thing for more than an instant.

Let's try another example: say you suddenly feel a flash of anger at your partner because once again she didn't put the top back on the toothpaste tube, even though you've asked her to do so many times. You shout, "I hate it when you do that!" As soon as you shout, you remember this suggestion, and do your best to notice what's happening. You notice the typical sensations of anger: heat rising in your chest and face, the distance between your righteous point of view and your partner's behavior, a near-immediate flood of mental justifications for raising your voice, etc. Now watch what happens. Either your point of view gets reinforced by more justifications (e.g., recounting all the previous wrong-doings of your partner), or it immediately starts to dissipate, naturally, on its own, if you don't add fuel to its fire.

This natural dissipating is sometimes called the "self-liberating" quality of phenomena.

The Dzogchen recognition of "release at inception" points to the same quality. In the words of Dzogchen teacher/translator Keith Dowman, *release at inception* entails "confidence in the simultaneity

of the inception and release of thought that induces a constant opening up that turns into seamless thought-free openness." And as
Longchenpa describes it:

> Whatever occurs externally as the manifold appearance of the
> five types of external objects (forms, sounds, smells, tastes and
> tangibles) or internally as some mental activity, at the very mo-
> ment of its inception as a field it is seen just as it is, and by
> the force of its advent it is fully potentiated and then vanishes
> by itself — how could it possibly remain? — released without
> a trace, and in that moment the three crucial functions —
> carefree detachment in whatever arises, access to wide-open
> spaciousness, and easy relaxation into the appearance upon its
> inception — are assimilated.[17]

It is not necessary to understand everything referred to by
Longchenpa in this passage right now. The important thing is simply
to begin to explore and appreciate, through your own experience,
that every perception that arises in your awareness, whether thought,
emotion, or sensation, "vanishes by itself." When we no longer put
energy into repeating mental phenomena, they vanish! This is the
natural release of fixations.

Through the constant practice of relaxing the grip of our attractions, aversions, and the reactive fixations that express themselves
from our preferences, we open to a serenity in our lives that allows
us to accept each experience as it arises — simply because that's
what's happening — without turbulent reactivity.

Rather than *losing* anything through releasing attachment to our
likes and dislikes, our experience opens us to the possibility of the
most profound intimacy.

A final example: imagine you are on your death bed. You know
you have only an hour or two left in this life. Your closest friend is

beside you. What would be most helpful to you in that moment? Would it be your friend responding to your imminent death with emotional reactivity from layers of fixations about loss, fear of death, attachment to you, etc.? Or would it be more helpful if your friend were serene, free of fixations, and completely present to you in those moments, accepting what is?

Exercises: Noticing Mental Constructions and Fixations

1. Observing Fixations

The purpose of this exercise is to become more aware of your fixations as they arise. The primary instruction is this: *over the coming weeks do whatever you can to observe your fixations and the attractions and aversions that motivate them.* Remember, you don't have to make value judgments here; you don't have to attack your attractions and aversions or judge them. Just notice them. Become an expert on your fixations. It is definitely helpful to fully acknowledge and accept that you — like all of us — have developed constellations of fixations over the course of your life that form your opinions, values, and belief systems. There is no need to hide them from yourself, or think you are a failure because you feel you are subject to them.

As mentioned in this chapter, you may choose to begin this exercise by noticing when you are constructing something — a set of justifications or some other interpretation. You may continue this process with a deeper inquiry, asking: From what attraction or aversion does this fixation arise?

Conversely, you may find it easier to directly take note of your tendencies of liking and disliking moment to moment. Watch what you approve of and what you don't approve of.

Continue this exercise by using the list of typical "fixation-situations" on pages _____ to expand the scope of your explorations.

Be aware that you may experience some resistance to this process because you may feel it makes you self-conscious or self-critical. If that's the case, then explore that feeling. Is there a fixation here?

This is an exercise in becoming aware of the presence of your preferences, opinions, and judgments. All you need to do is to notice them — you don't have to psychoanalyze yourself or change the way you react — just make a little space between your liking or disliking something and the reaction that arises from that liking or disliking. In that space you will be able to notice what's happening.

2. Fixation Dialogue

This exercise is most easily done with a partner, at least to begin with. Ask a friend who is open to this kind of exploration to join you; perhaps you can explain your understanding of this chapter to them, or ask them to read it. If working with a partner is not possible, you can still engage in this dialogue; simply take both parts yourself. At some point you will internalize this kind of dialogue anyway, inquiring into the nature of fixations directly without the need for a partner. If you feel reluctant to work with someone in this way, or with yourself, perhaps thinking, *I am too busy, the other person will be too busy, I'd rather wait and do this later, this won't work for me, this is a ridiculous exercise, etc.*, notice these are fixations! Notice your preferences here and the level they are working in you. In a couple of months you will be glad you did.

This exercise introduces what Buddhists call *unfindability inquiry* — the main topic of the next chapter. In this exercise we will begin with just one element of the inquiry process; engaging with it now will make the next stage of our work unfold more easily.

The phenomenon of fixation is a relational event: it has three elements: (1) someone who is fixated (the fixator); (2) some thought, belief, feeling, event, etc., to which they are fixated (the fixation); and (3) the process of fixation itself, how it works (the fixating). A strange aspect of this process is that if we look closely at any one of these elements, the object of our inquiry dissolves before our eyes.

Here we will focus specifically on number three — the process of fixating — asking: What is it? Where does it happen? How exactly do we "fix" or grasp or cling to this fixation? How is it stuck onto us?

In this exercise there are two roles: the *fixator* and the *inquirer*. Take each role in turn with your partner (or yourself if alone). Here are the instructions:

The *fixator* speaks of a personal fixation — something he or she holds onto such as an ideal, an anxiety, an image of him or herself, a possession, a past experience. This exercise works best when the fixation is currently being experienced *in the moment*; otherwise the inquiry can become theoretical and abstract. To help this, the inquirer may ask their partner to try to "generate" the feeling of the fixation, or find one that is readily experienced in the moment.

The *inquirer* listens carefully, respecting that your partner's report is indeed what he or she is experiencing, while at the same time genuinely curious about how this is actually happening. Your task now is to initiate an inquiry with your partner that questions the assumption that the fixation has some kind of property by which it "sticks" to the fixator.

Types of questions you might use are: Can you contact in yourself how this (past experience, etc.) holds onto you? Can you locate where it is happening? Is it happening now? Does it hold onto you, or do you hold onto it? How does it do that? Or how do you do that? Are you doing it now? Do you hold onto it with a thought? How do you stick the thought to the fixation? Can you show me how you do that? Other questions will surface. Allow them to rise naturally, giving plenty of time for introspection.

Be creative with your questions. See where it goes. Notice if you get caught up in the construction of your partner's fixation. Don't be concerned if you do. Do this long enough so the inquiry is authentically experienced, but don't labor it toward any kind of conclusion. This last point is important — avoid the feeling that you or your partner has to accomplish something or have a breakthrough. This is simply an open-ended and honest inquiry, without a goal.

Of course this is a very odd series of questions — and once you have read through these instructions you may think you get the point and there's no need to do the exercise. Nevertheless I encourage you to try this, and to try to answer the questions posed to you. What is the internal dynamic by which you attach to a fixation?

3. Meditation Practice

Sitting in silence "doing nothing" and "doing your practices" are excellent fields in which to continue this exercise of observing your fixations. Here are two approaches:

1   If you have been giving time each day to *the practice of subtle opening* (chapter two) or other meditation practices, during your practice time observe closely your likes and dislikes, and your desire to have your experience change or remain the same. Watch carefully when you start feeling your present experience should change, or that you want it to keep happening as it is at that moment. Notice the root impulses of restlessness, boredom, the desire for stimulation, and the desire for more meaning (or, conversely, the desire for mental silence).

Notice how you sense these impulses when they occur. Be curious about the arising and passing of your impatience.

2   During your meditation practice, watch how mental constructions may begin to assemble in your consciousness. Become aware of your interest in them and how they form fixations. Watch what happens to them when you notice them.

· 5 ·

SELF-INQUIRY

Self-inquiry is a style of radical questioning that deconstructs fixations. This type of inquiry can relax the grip of habitual "self-positioning" that is at the root of all fixations: e.g., being the one who approves of this and disapproves of that, the one who is unhappy, or happy, or lost, or unworthy, or worthy, etc. As our identification with these "self-positions" evaporates, the possibility opens for unfiltered recognition of our true nature.

This chapter introduces two lines of approach in self-inquiry: (1) questions that encourage us to make contact with the somatic experience — the physical sensations — that lurk at the root of the fixation-making process; and (2) questions that lead to the recognition that each element of the fixation-making process is fundamentally insubstantial and unfindable.

These lines of self-inquiry are effective because they help undermine our belief in the logic of a particular fixation. Self-inquiry turns our attention to noticing *what is actually happening now*, or *what is true right now* — either in terms of energetic, sensate experience, or the direct recognition of pure, contentless awareness.

It is important to note that this kind of self-inquiry is not meant to replace psychotherapy. Its purpose is not to heal a person's psychological wounds or traumatic experiences, or enhance one's coping skills. These kinds of things may indeed occur in some cases, but to engage in this work with the expectation of such results would be a mistake. I feel it is especially important for us to recognize when psychotherapy may be appropriate, and to not be shy about engaging in it or encouraging others to do so.

Self-inquiry has a different purpose. It employs a type of simple questioning aimed at loosening our belief in the idea that we are a separate self. It does this, as I mentioned above, by remaining faithful to the questions: *What is happening right now?* and *What is true right now?* The rootedness of self-inquiry in the here and now is essential, because it cuts through thought constructions and emotionally laden stories built of memory of the past and projections of the future. Coming into the present moment and recognizing what is actually happening allows our awareness to "relax into" its own nature, prior to any content.

Forms of self-inquiry don't follow a neat recipe. The actual questions posed are changeable according to the person and the circumstances, although certain questions do tend to recur. Rather, the effectiveness of self-inquiry depends upon the clarity and equanimity of the questioner. But don't let this intimidate you — in my experience one of the best ways to deepen our capacity for recognizing and stabilizing the experience of spontaneously present awareness is to engage in this type of inquiry both as the questioner and the one questioned.

The forms of questioning described here are drawn from major nondual traditions: the Hindu sages of *Advaita Vedanta*; the koans of the Zen Rinzai tradition, the *unfindability inquiry* of the Buddhist sage Nagarjuna; the pointing out questions of the Tibetan Buddhist Mahamudra tradition; and the various inquiry processes illustrated in the writings and satsangs of contemporary nondual teachers such as Jean Klein, Sri Nisargadatta Maharaj, Bob Adamson, Peter Fenner, John Wheeler, Tony Parsons, Isaac Shapiro, Karl Renz, and Adyashanti.

In the examples described here, self-inquiry is presented mainly as a conversation that happens between two people: a questioner or guide and the person being questioned. However, these forms of questioning can easily be internalized and used productively on your own.

THE RESONANT FIELD

In work between two people, self-inquiry requires creating a shared space in which the questioner sees the one questioned not as a troubled or confused person, but in his or her fundamental nature as open, pure awareness. In the view of the questioner there is no separation between him or herself and the person being questioned. This shared space allows the questioner to "feel from the inside" the nature of the dissonance between what the person experiences is real and *what actually is.*

A field of resonance occurs through the coming together of several factors: the clarity of open awareness in which the guide rests; the guide's skill with the inquiry process; the readiness and sincerity of the one being questioned; and the safety and undistracted quality of the environment in which the inquiry occurs.

The resonant field is best served when the questioner/guide is free from any agenda and is not pushing for a specific outcome. If the person being questioned experiences some level of liberation from a fixation, that's fine. If not, that's okay too. This equanimity in the guide is helpful to the person being questioned, especially by reducing the sense that the guide is going to "do" something that will affect change from the outside, or that an expectation is placed on the person questioned that he or she must "get it." Then the person is free to engage directly with what is happening, without pressure.

THE ONE RULE

"The One Rule" is a name I've given to a simple dynamic in self-inquiry: when working with your own fixation or guiding another's inquiry with a fixation, *move attention toward the actual physical sensations occurring in the moment that signal the presence of the fixation.* This means that in the inquiry process one gently encourages a person to turn their attention to the physical sensations that appear prior to interpreting them as "fear" or "anxiety" or "anger" or any other named emotion, or any causative stories associated with the fixation in question. The person is instead invited to focus on the actual sensations they feel in the moment — their location, qualities, and intensity, and then simply experience them without interpretation.

This process works best when the person doing the work is actually experiencing the affect of their fixation in the moment, rather than thinking about a fixation they have been disturbed by in the past, or expect to be disturbed by in the future. However, if one is not experiencing the affect of the fixation during the inquiry process, and is more or less reporting about the fixation from memory, this practice can still be useful since it familiarizes one with recognizing the physical sensations associated with the fixation.

In describing this process to someone who asked how she might overcome her fear, Jean Klein remarked:

> Find out and explore the actual perception, the sensation of fear, where it is localized in your body, its density and so on. In discovering the percept you are disassociated from it. In exploring what you are not, you discover what you are.

To give us a more concrete example of the dynamics of self-inquiry, let's create an imaginary dialogue between yourself and the woman Jean Klein was responding to. Let's say she tells you that she is often fearful in social situations, unsure of herself, and anxious.

You might begin by asking:

This fear that you are describing, are you feeling it now?
"Yes."

I'd like to invite you to get in contact with this feeling, can you do that? (Pause)
"OK, yes, it's quite strong now."

Can you describe where it is in your body that you sense it?
"It's in my chest somehow, around my heart."

Can you describe the feeling itself, the actual sensation — is it hot, or cold, or like a pressure or pain, a dull ache or a sharp ache?
"It's more like a feeling of compression, a clenching, and a feeling of dread."

What is this "dread" feeling? How does it show up in your body? Is it the same clenching feeling in your chest, or something different? (Pause) (Notice here that the questioner spotted the word "dread," which is an emotional interpretation just like the word "fear," and inquired into its actual physical sensation in the moment, rather than have the person get tangled in the mental interpretation signified by the word "dread.")
"It's sort of a hollowness inside the compression, inside the clenching."

Is it uncomfortable?
"Very uncomfortable. It's awful."

Okay, this awful feeling, this hollowness inside the clenching feel-
ing, can you invite it into your awareness, just let it be there in its
raw feeling?

Here you want to gently encourage the person to stay with the
feeling they describe, however uncomfortable. Prevent yourself from
talking too much at this point, or trying to comfort or offer expla-
nations of what is happening. However, it is often helpful if, once
in a while, you repeat the words the person used to describe the feeling — in this case, "compression," "clenching," "hollowness inside
the clenching" — to help them stay with it. You may also repeat the
words like this, and then ask, *Are these feelings still there, or have they*
changed? This allows the person to check in the moment to notice
what is actually happening, rather than pursuing the idea of a feeling
that is no longer present.

The dynamic at work here is that the fixation is being linked directly to its root sensations, and is then held in the light of awareness.
The painful, preverbal energy of the fixation is being experienced
steadily rather than avoided.

Let's return now to our imaginary inquiry:

How are you doing now? Is that hollow, clenching feeling still in
your chest?
   "Yes. It's very strong."

On a scale from one to ten, what number would you give the in-
tensity of this sensation — ten being the most severe?
   "Eight."

OK. Just stay with it, just allow that sensation to take center stage
in your awareness. If it changes or moves, feel free to tell me what's
happening. Can you do that?
   "Yes." (Long pause.)

What's happening now?

"It's moved down; it's now more in my solar plexus."

Can you describe the feeling? Is it still compressed, with hollowness inside?

"No, it's different now. It feels more like an old ache, a lonesome feeling."

Stay with the direct sensation. This lonesome feeling, what is it? What is the sensation that shows it?

"It's changing. Getting more dispersed, like the ache feeling is getting thinner."

If you gave it a number right now, what would it be?

"More like a five, or a four."

OK, stay with it, just allow it your full attention as it moves or stays. (Long pause) …What's happening now?

"I don't exactly know."

Is the ache or the clenching-hollow feeling still around? Can you locate it somewhere?

"Only a little. Actually I feel much calmer. What happened?"

Sometimes following the One Rule in an inquiry results in a happy "conclusion," as in our imaginary conversation above. But remember there is no need to push it to a happy conclusion — just let the experience follow its own movement and timing. Most often, the sensations described tend to move in the body, sometimes becoming more intense for a while, even producing severe emotional states: tears, shaking, etc. If these occur, as a questioner just stay in close contact without trying to console the person or distract them. Let the stuck energy get released, for this is what is happening: what we are calling "fixations" often get lodged in the body as uncomfortable feelings the person wants to protect himself or herself from. When you invite these feelings into awareness in this supportive way, these stuck energies are allowed to move and resolve without the need to analyze them or delve into the stories that have been associated with them. This is the natural healing of open awareness.

A variant on this kind of self-inquiry can involve some suggestions of release, rather than letting the stuck energies move of their own accord. Here the questioner may ask the person if he or she can sense "the space around" the sensation they are reporting. (This is best done after the sensation is well-established in the person's attention.) Again, it is important to go slowly at this point. In effect, the sensation is being localized as an object in space, and this "space" noticed. Then the questioner asks the person if they can allow the sensation (the hollow feeling, the clenched feeling, the burning feeling, the ache, etc.) to slowly dissolve into the space around it. Another possibility here is to ask the person, *Are you in the sensation you are reporting, or are you in the space around it?* This is a kind of shortcut you can use with almost any fixation or thought pattern.

The One Rule can be especially helpful in one's own practice. The same process applies: as you notice you are caught in the whirlpool of a story, allow yourself to experience directly the sensations that give rise to it. Watch how you tend to elaborate on the reasons for the fixation (and its sensations) rather than simply sitting with the discomfort. Let yourself feel it. Watch how the uncomfortable sensations change. Repeat this every time you are aware the fixation is recycling in your thoughts. You may notice in some cases that you resist continuing this process because you are not 100 percent sure you want to be rid of the fixation. This is an important discovery!

After a while you may find that when a familiar fixation begins recycling or elaborating in your thoughts, you notice this and are no longer hooked by the energetic discomfort at its root, because it has lost its insistence. At that point you can simply turn your attention to the recycling thoughts and, unconcerned with their content, question their substantiality, as described in the following section.

UNFINDABILITY

In the "Fixation Dialogue" exercise at the end of the last chapter, you were introduced to this form of self-inquiry, which is known as *unfindability inquiry* in Zen. It has its origins in the Madhyamaka tradition that arose from the teachings of the great second-century Buddhist master Nagarjuna, and was further elaborated in the Tibetan Mahamudra tradition as exemplified by the sixteenth-century master Dakpo Rashi Namgyal. Here we will consider this form of inquiry in more detail, since it is a potent approach to loosening habits of mind and self-concepts.

As mentioned in chapter four, fixation is a relational event. There are three elements involved in this relation: (1) someone who "has" the fixation (the fixator); (2) some thought, belief, or feeling to which they are fixated (the fixation); and (3) the process or glue by which the fixator is fixed to the fixation (the identification).

It is useful to categorize these three areas simply to help you, as a questioner, shift among them. There is no need, however, to exhaust one series of questions around one element before moving to the next. They may be explored interchangeably as appropriate. As with the One Rule, you may engage this form of inquiry with a partner, or, if you don't have one, internalize the questions suggested here as you explore the nature of your own fixations. It is helpful to have a fixation in mind as you read along — for example, "I don't feel at ease," or "I am confused," or "I miss my youth," etc.

The type of questions raised regarding *the first element* — the fixator — challenge the identity and reality of the subject. Here are a few of many possible examples:

- *Can you describe who it is who is having these thoughts (feelings)?*
- *Can you point to where this "I" is?*
- *Does it have a physical location?*
- *Does it take up space?*
- *This "I" that we keep referring to, what exactly is it?*
- *What is it made out of?*
- *How do you experience it?*
- *How do you distinguish it from something else?*
- *Does it have an outer edge? A color? A texture?*
- *Who are you?*
- *What are you?*
- *Are you different from how you were ten years ago?*
- *If you are different, then how do you know you are still "you?"*
- *If you are not different, what is it that stays the same?*
- *Does that which stays the same have any qualities or attributes that you can describe?*

The point of these questions, and the ones described below, is less to evince a definitive answer and more to produce, we might say, a sense of bewilderment. The idea is to loosen the ingrained assumptions of one's identity as a person, and even more penetratingly, to loosen one's identity as a fixed entity of any kind. As you will quickly see when you try this, there is no one way the inquiry process goes. It's important to stay flexible and creative, and engage in the inquiry with the qualities of immediacy and curiosity. Avoid being aggressive with your questions.

In a similar way, we can posit questions around *the second element* — the thought, belief, or feeling that forms the content of the fixation. Possible lines of inquiry here are:

- *This issue that troubles you — is it a thought?*
- *If so, are you thinking it now?*
- *Is it an image?*
- *What happens when you don't think it (or see it) — where is it? Does it still exist?*
- *Does it exist only when you think about it?*
- *Or if it always exists, where do you keep it when you are not aware of it?*
- *Or is it a feeling?*
- *If it is a feeling, what happens to it when you are feeling something else? Does it still exist?*
- *Are you feeling it now? If so, can you tell if it has a beginning, middle, and end? Or does it not happen in time that way?*
- *Does it occur in space like this chair?*
- *If so, can you point to where it is occurring?*
- *Is this issue that troubles you about something that has happened in the past?*
- *If so, where is it now?*
- *Is it about something that will happen in the future?*
- *If so, where is it now?*
- *Is it about something that is happening now?*
- *If so, where is it? Can you show it to me?*

In my experience, inquiry into the experiential nature of a fixation often results in reports that the fixation is sensed in the body — as a contraction, heat, tingling, pressure, etc. When that occurs, you may wish to go to the inquiry process described under the One Rule and let exploration of this raw energy take precedence.

When this isn't the case, the inquiry works at loosening assumptions around the substantiality of the person's thoughts, beliefs, and feelings. He or she finds they are unable to answer any of these questions definitively. There arises an odd realization that they have been functioning "inside" an assemblage of thought constructions that

are not verifiable or consistent. Here again, rather than finding answers to this line of questioning, the person may simply experience
bewilderment. The inconclusive nature of the self-inquiry process is
its point.

For example, let's imagine a person reported feeling troubled by
a fear of death. You begin engaging them in a process of inquiry
using some of the questions listed above. There may be a moment
or two of exasperation on the part of the person questioned, whether
expressed or unexpressed, that might go something like: *Yes, it is a
feeling, but no, I can't point to it. It's not like that. It doesn't take up
space like a chair. But it's real to me! Of course it's about something that
will happen in the future. No, it's not happening now, but the feeling of
fear could be happening now, even though right now it isn't. Oh, I see.
I'm afraid of feeling, in the future, the fear that I will die, in the future.*

Sometimes, at a point like this, you might suggest that the person
do whatever she or he could do to generate that feeling, in this case
the fear of death. Usually people say they know how to make themselves feel it. Go slow here and encourage the generation of the fixation. Inquire into their process as needed — encourage them to see
for themselves the pattern of thinking involved in the production of
the feeling. This "seeing" is precious in itself.

Remember, no conclusions are necessary. The loosening of assumptions is the point.

Again, with *the third element* — the process or glue by which the
fixator is fixed to the fixation — we play with a line of questions that
may serve to loosen the assumptions surrounding the insistence of
the fixation's affect. For example, you might ask:

- *You say you can't let go of this feeling. Can you show me how
  you are holding on to it?*
- *Or is it holding on to you?*
- *Is it happening now? How do you know?*

- *Do you hold on to it with your thoughts?*
- *If so, how does the thought stick to this feeling (fixation)?*
- *I'm curious about how this happens — how it works that this feeling keeps recurring and what mechanism it uses to do that. Can you describe it?*
- *What exactly is happening when it comes back and sticks to you?*
- *To what part of you does it stick? Etc.*

Here we can see how the odd playfulness of the inquiry questions the very structure of our thought processes and our root assumptions about what we are and what is happening. At its root, this line of questioning refers back to the insubstantial nature of the "I" and reveals it. The whole mental representation of a "self" that "has" "fixations" may be seen through. We can no more find the fixation than we can find the self, or how the fixation vexes the self.

FURTHER LINES OF SELF-INQUIRY

Gradually we can extend this type of self-inquiry into other beliefs that are propped up by unquestioned assumptions. For example, we might inquire into the reality of the thought *I am my body.* To begin, we might scan the statement for its core concepts: (1) there is an entity called "I"; (2) this entity possesses something, namely a body; (3) not only does it possess this body, it is also *identical* with the body (signified by the word "am.") If we can look at these core concepts from the nonreferential view of nondual awareness, we might ask questions such as the following:

1. THE "I"
   - *Who is it that is "my body?"*
   - *What do you look like without your body?*

- *If you possess a body (signified by the possessive pronoun "my") how can you also be that body?*
- *Are you this body I see now?*
- *If so, what about the body you had when you were ten years old? Was that you too?*
- *But that body was different, so you must have been different too.*
- *Was it a different "I" then, or the same as the "I" that is now?*
- *And where is this "I" located?*
- *Is it somewhere inside the body, or is it the whole body?*
- *If it's the whole body and you lose a leg, would your "I" be less?*
- *If the "I" is somewhere inside your body, how big is it?*
- *Does it have edges? If so, what does it look like? Etc.*

2. My Body
- *What is this body that you are?*
- *Can you define its border?*
- *Is it your skin?*
- *Certainly if your skin wasn't there the body would perish, so the border of your body must be the skin. But if there was no atmosphere to breathe, the body would also perish, so does your body's border include the atmosphere?*
- *If there was no sun in the sky your body would also perish, so does its border include the sun?*
- *This body must have food, otherwise it will disintegrate, so is it also its food?*
- *For its food to be produced there must be a farmer who grows it, so is your body also the farmer? The field? Etc.*

3. I <u>am</u> my body.
- *How do you "am" — that is, how do you exist?*
- *Is it something you do?*

- *Or does it just happen to you?*
- *To whom does it happen?*
- *How does it happen?*
- *Will it stop?*
- *How do you know it will stop?*
- *What exactly does it mean to "be?"*
- *How do you know when "being" is happening — by what signs do you know it?*
- *How will you know when it stops happening? Etc.*

There are many ways to explore this kind of deconstructive self-inquiry. Learn to become creative with it. Play. Assume nothing. The open and transparent ground of being, the clear radiance that is our natural state, does not reveal itself through the lens of assumptions. We have to leave our identifications, fixations, and beliefs behind.

Constantly deconstructing, investigating keenly,
Not even the slightest substance can be found;
And in the undivided moment of nondual perception
We abide in the natural state of perfection.[18]

—LONGCHENPA

Exercises: Self-Inquiry

Explore working with each of the types of self-inquiry described in this chapter — if possible with a partner to begin with, and then directly with yourself. Once you have established some familiarity with these exercises, self-inquiry can be used with great effectiveness when fixation reactions arise in daily life.

Become sensitive to when it is appropriate to work with *the One Rule:* moving attention toward the actual physical sensations occurring in the moment that signal the presence of the fixation.

Practice becoming creative with the several approaches to *unfindability inquiry.*

Over time, develop your capacity for self-inquiry so that it becomes more and more natural to you. Become skilled at tracking what is actually happening in the moment, rather than settling for thoughts about what is happening. This skill is the key to all self-inquiry.

Be careful to approach these forms of self-inquiry in a spirit of sincerity and good will toward yourself and those you are working with. Students of nondual teachings sometimes fall into a casual style of speaking that uses nondual jargon, or self-inquiry questions, superficially or out of context. While lightheartedness is wonderful, there is no need to play "gotcha" as we help each other see through assumptions and fractional points of view.

When you're engaging in self-inquiry with yourself, invite it into every possible situation in your life. When you're engaging in self-inquiry with another person, however, take care to do it only after having established a resonant field — a safe, shared space in which the questioner sees the one questioned not as a troubled or confused person, but in his or her fundamental nature as open, pure awareness. The more experience one has in creating (and honoring) the resonant field — both as inquirer and inquiree — the more quickly and effortlessly it is created.

You may find that you don't quite know how to start an inquiry process with a partner. This is because we are treating self-inquiry here as a practice or exercise, rather than as a natural response to someone — or yourself — struggling with a fixation reaction. Because this is an exercise, you or your partner will have to come up with an issue, a fixation, that can serve as the basis for the inquiry. Sometimes this is easy — an issue is current for one of you and can be experienced in the moment without too much effort.

If this is not the case, you might try asking a leading question such as: *What is happening for you right now?* or *What are you feeling about doing this exercise?* or *What are you experiencing now in response to your study of nonduality?*

Let's say your partner answers one of these questions, "I am feeling self-conscious about doing self-inquiry with you." Now you have the makings of a fixation: (1) the fixator, "I;" (2) the fixation, "self-consciousness;" and (3) how the two are connected, the fixating, the "am feeling." You can start with any of these elements, remembering to keep the inquiry in present moment experience as much as possible: e.g., *Are you feeling self-conscious right now? Can you describe what that feels like? Look carefully at this feeling of self-consciousness. When you look at it, can you find it?* And so on.

The only effective way to explore self-inquiry with someone is to open yourself into the spacious identitylessness of your natural state, and inquire from that spaciousness. This also allows you to recognize the spacious identitylessness of your partner's intrinsic nature, even though he or she may be struggling with a nonspacious sense of their identity in the moment.

A Few Contemplations on the Open Path

I encourage you to pause now in your reading of this book, and give a few days to contemplating the suggestions and questions you'll find on the next four pages. Let each of these contemplations become yours, as if the voice that is speaking them is your own.

The work we are doing here requires direct recognition. This is different from simply reading a text and gathering its information, and agreeing or disagreeing with what is said. Direct recognition means coming to an intuition of something first-hand, not from second-hand descriptions. The contemplations suggested on the next four pages are designed to help you open in this way.

Although these contemplations are expressed in words, your responses to them may not be. If this occurs, relax naturally and allow yourself to open into the source of this wordless response.

Take all the time you need for these. Return to them as often as you feel to, even after you continue reading and doing future exercises in this book.

CONTEMPLATIONS ON WHAT YOU ARE

Notice when you wake in the morning, the open quality of your presence.

Notice when you are washing your body, the emptiness of your simply being here.

Notice when you are preparing food, the stillness at the origin of your actions.

Notice when you are in conversation with someone, the silence that listens.

Notice that whatever is now taking place in your mind, you are untouched by it.

Can you find yourself?

Can you find your thoughts?

Can you find your feelings?

If you can find any of these, are they now where you found them?

If you cannot find any of these, what are you without them?

CONTEMPLATIONS ON CHOICE AND ACTION

Can you discover the difference between trying to do something and doing it?

Will you *try* to discover the difference, or will you do it? How will you know the difference?

Can you do something you don't want to do? Try.

Choose to do a simple act like moving your hand. Can you find the origin of the "choice?"

Recall an important life decision you made in the past.

Is there any evidence that you could have made a different choice?

If your answer is yes, wouldn't that different choice then have been made?

Look closely at the choices you make during the day, like deciding what to wear, or what to eat, or decisions in your work. Ask: what chooses? Look carefully to see what it is that chooses, and how that happens.

Whatever is now taking place in your mind, have you chosen that?

CONTEMPLATIONS ON ATTACHMENT AND NONATTACHMENT
Consider all the things in your life you have to lose. Name some of them to yourself.

Now consider how it is you "have" them. By what means do you possess them? How are you connected to them?

Are the things in your life that you could lose here now?

If they are not, in what way do you have them now?

If they are, in what way do you have them now? For example, if you say "I have my life now, and I could lose it," investigate how it is you "have" your life now. And what is it you have? And what has it?

Explore finding the space in which you have nothing to lose.

Consider how this space is different from the normal space of your life in which you have things to lose.

CONTEMPLATIONS ON BEING IN THE MOMENT

If you ask what is happening now,
and then wait a few seconds and ask again —
what is happening now —
you will notice that what is happening in both cases is not the same.
Is anything the same?
What?

Let yourself relax in this moment, completely relax.
In this state of relaxation, what is it that is relaxed?

If you notice anything that is not relaxed in this moment, what is it?
Is it a nonrelaxation in your body? Thoughts? Feelings? Memories? Something else?

If you have found something that is not relaxed, look carefully at it.
Is it an essential, permanent part of you, or does it come and go?

Ask: am I present in this moment?
If your answer is no, then where are you?
If your answer is yes, then ask: what is present?

Can you find the past?
The future?
The present?

In the transparency of this moment, ask:
do I really know what will happen next?

If your answer is yes, ask: how do I know?

If your answer is no, ask: am I at peace with that?

Notice what is occurring spontaneously now. Rest in that awareness.

· 6 ·

MOTIVATION AND EFFORTLESSNESS

*Only when we live in our wholeness, free from the person, free
from all goals, preference and choice, can there be a full expression
of life. When we live without qualifying we live in the moment,
the eternal present "now." Here, in the absence of thoughts of the
past and longings for the future, we are in our fullness. From fullness flows love and all actions come out of love.*

—JEAN KLEIN

AN OVERVIEW

Let's take a moment to review the journey we have begun in the first
five chapters of this book.

In chapter one we acknowledged our purpose: to recognize the
spontaneous presence of clear, open awareness that is our intrinsic
nature and the ground of all being. We saw that this term — "open
awareness" — is synonymous with many other terms used in the

world's mystical traditions to indicate the ultimate goal of all spiritual endeavor: illumination, primordial mind, unconditional love, God-consciousness, enlightenment, the oneness of being, Buddha nature, etc. As we began to talk about "it," we discovered that "it" eludes all definition and confounds any attempt of our minds to grasp it. And yet it is right here, now, in the heart of everything that is occurring; there is nowhere we need to go to find it, and nothing we need to do to make it happen. This realization — that there is nowhere we need to go and nothing we need to do — remains true at every moment, yet we also sense that we are indeed traveling a path. Such is the curious paradox at the center of the Open Path: *there is nowhere to go, yet steps are taken.*

Chapter two introduced the "practice of subtle opening," a basic meditation that helps to calm our thoughts and emotions, reveals to us the transparent, ungraspable nature of timeless awareness, and welcomes us to the ease of the "non-meditation" of simply doing nothing. Combining aspects of mindfulness and breathing meditations, devotion, mind-calming, visualization, *zikr*, mantra, and what is known in Zen as *shikantaza* ("just sitting") the practice of subtle opening relaxes the mental and emotional urgencies of our conditioning. Of course, once again it is important to remember that realization of open awareness does not come as a result of this or any other practice — yet by practicing in this way we are creating the conditions in which direct realization may be more likely.

In chapter three we explored how recognition of the infinite presence of open awareness can be obscured by the many ways we sustain the illusion of being a separate self: through constant busyness, through identifying our "self" as the one who likes or dislikes things, who wills and controls things, who knows things and makes meaning, or who is possessed by hope and fear.

Chapter four introduced the notion of mental constructions and fixations — biased attitudes that distort our view of reality. We began to notice the signs of fixations as they arise, such as self-defensive-ness, self-pity, complaints, annoyance, assertive opinions, etc. We also became familiar with the recognition that at the core of these biased attitudes is the belief that *I am a personal, separate self* defined by my likes and dislikes, a being who is in charge of my thoughts and emotions, and, to some extent, who is in charge of what happens. An important part of our work has been, and will continue to be, to inquire into the evidence behind these core beliefs of our identity. We also considered that the most reliable way to release fixations is simply by *seeing* them, noticing them, becoming aware of the patterns of identification as they arise. No analysis or effort to eradicate is necessary. If we make this gentle noticing the "practice" of our life, gradually ingrained patterns of reactivity and identification disappear.

In chapter five we explored the process of self-inquiry, giving us further tools for releasing our fixed attitudes and assumptions. Here we saw how we might follow the "One Rule" — remaining present to the actual sensations that arise in our bodies when we react from fixed patterns of thought and emotion. We also explored styles of inquiry that reveal the *unfindability* of the various elements within our fixations. Not being able to find these elements upon which we base so many of our beliefs and actions, we are released into the possibility of experiencing the world and ourselves freshly.

In summarizing our journey in this way, it may sound like there is a lot to do to loosen the bonds of these "ingrained patterns of reactivity and identification." And yes, we could look at it that way — I don't want to trivialize what we are facing here. Sufis call this process *unlearning,* and it is classically understood to be extremely challenging. At the same time, it is refreshing to realize that the unlearning we are engaged in always happens instantaneously and effortlessly. We simply let go. The invitation of this work is, finally, an invitation to relax our lives into the clear openness of being, unadorned by attachment to personal or societal stories. It is welcoming the ever-present freshness of open awareness, our natural state, now.

In this chapter we will consider the spirit with which we approach this work. To begin with, we will look at our *motivation*. What is our real motivation for doing this work? Upon what is our motivation based? Related to motivation may be an inner experience of *longing*. Does our longing for union with the Divine deepen our engagement with this work, or does our longing create further obstacles by becoming an experience unto itself? We will also reflect on our inner *attitude* — the way in which we hold ourselves as we engage with these methods of awakening — and begin our contemplation of *effortlessness*, a key to both inviting direct recognition and sustaining it throughout our lives.

MOTIVATION

First let us consider our motivation. Why do we do this work? When we feel our initial enthusiasm for nondual awakening diminish, what energy draws us back to our practices and self-inquiry? What calls us back to our study, discussion, and creativity with this subtle process? It can seem so insubstantial, all this talk of openness and selflessness! Is it worth it? Will we get anything out of it? Will it make us happier?

Perhaps we have been drawn to this work by the idea of enlightenment, having read or heard enough mystical teachings to sense that recognition of "clear empty awareness" is essential for that spiritual project. Perhaps we want to enjoy the "bliss of pure being" that we have heard about. Perhaps we simply want to be released from the tedium of our life, or from the more serious burdens of our life's sufferings. We may have explored in our life a number of different approaches to spiritual experience and expression, and feel we have come to their limits.

While nothing is inherently wrong with any of these motivations, we can nevertheless recognize in stating them like this that they are all rooted in a *gaining idea*. We want a result. We want enlightenment. We want bliss. We want freedom from suffering. We want to show up to others as realized beings.

As long as we are propelled in our practice by the idea of gaining something, we are locked into the expectations of time — that there will be some realization or experience in the future that will one day appear to us as a result of our practice. Time-bound consciousness, however, cannot conceive of clear empty awareness. Thus our linear expectation guarantees we will remain within its linear logic, and never "arrive."

A similar logic, and trap, can occur in the cultivation of spiritual *longing*. An emphasis on spiritual longing can be seen in those mystical traditions that have arisen in relation to a deity-centered or guru-centered religion. Such traditions include various forms of Jewish and Christian mysticism, Sufism, Hinduism, Tibetan Buddhism, Pure Land Buddhism, and indigenous shamanic traditions. In these approaches to "enlightenment," it is often evident that union with the Divine — whether God or guru — involves the projection of an ideal state toward which we aspire. Our desire to recognize the spontaneous presence of open awareness could become the same type of reification — a mystical romanticism — if we are not careful.

The contradiction inherent in these approaches is that my longing, by its very nature, keeps me separated from what I long for. We will return to the subject of longing later in this chapter, because it also holds a beautiful treasure, but for now it is enough to acknowledge that all motivation for traveling this path that is structured with a *gaining idea*, by definition must maintain the illusion of distance between the subject and its object, between the lover and the Beloved, until that gaining idea is relinquished.

Is there any source of motivation that is free of a gaining idea? Perhaps simply this: that we do this work *because we have to* — for no reason other than we cannot *not* do it. Those who don't *have to*, don't continue with it. We may think of some metaphysical explanation for our "having to," but in the end our desire is simply its own proof. Perhaps the most elegant way to describe this "having to" is the way Rumi does in the following poem:

> *A man goes to sleep in the town*
> *where he has always lived, and he dreams he's living*
> *in another town.*
>
> *In the dream, he doesn't remember*
> *the town he's sleeping in his bed in. He believes*
> *the reality of the dream town.*
>
> *The world is that kind of sleep.*
>
> *The dust of many crumbled cities*
> *settles over us like a forgetful doze,*
> *but we are older than those cities.*
>
> *We began*
> *as a mineral. We emerged into plant life*
> *and into the animal state, and then into being human,*
> *and always we have forgotten our former states,*
> *except in early spring when we slightly recall*
> *being green again.*

That's how a young person turns
toward a teacher. That's how a baby leans
toward the breast, without knowing the secret
of its desire, yet turning instinctively.

Humankind is being led along an evolving course,
through this migration of intelligences,
and though we seem to be sleeping,
there is an inner wakefulness
that directs the dream,

and that will eventually startle us back
to the truth of who we are...[19]

The message here is simple: let us allow our motivation for awakening to occur in the same way the baby leans toward the breast: "without knowing the secret of our desire."

And yet, there is something else. There is another layer to the mystery of why we do this work, although when we speak of it we may see it as another aspect of the "instinctive turning" pointed to in Rumi's poem. It has to do with what we might call *natural generosity.*

Up to now in this reflection we have been framing the question of motivation in terms of our own desire for enlightenment. This is understandable from the perspective of the separate self, from our conditioned sense that "we" are suffering or in darkness and therefore we long for light.

But as we know, the perspective of the separate self is distorted. It is a perspective we are all familiar with, one that produces gaining ideas and other anxieties about being incomplete. Released from this perspective of separateness we sense — without the need to think about it — that at the heart of our motivation for awakening is simply love.

Ultimately, we turn to this work not for our own sake but because we are inseparable from the awakening of life to itself. We do this for the sake of everything — which includes our loved ones, children yet to be born, all who suffer, everyone. We do it for the sake of this beautiful world. At first we may have to imagine this is true, but gradually we come to sense it *is* true. The most reliable motivation — if we need one — that helps our heart open when we feel ourselves contracting, is this desire to awaken for the sake of all. This is a strange and wonderful thing — it is not a "spiritual sentiment" but an occurrence of natural generosity, the grace intrinsic to each living moment.

ATTITUDE

Those of you who are familiar with the literature of nondual teachings will recognize the well-known controversy between two distinct schools of thought. Those who champion the need for *effort* on the path contend that there is a necessity for practices and methods to help us recognize the timeless, spontaneous presence of awareness, while those who speak for *effortlessness*, maintain that there is nothing to practice, that nothing needs to be done, and that what we seek is already here. (This paradox is expressed in the name *Open Path* itself, since a *path* is a specific, defined route to travel, while *openness* is not limited by any definition or boundary.)

Adherents of the gradual, progressive path assert that training is necessary because most people are entangled in the illusion of separateness and fixations, and breaking free from those tangles — even if they are fundamentally illusory — requires sincere attention and sustained effort. In contrast, adherents of the direct path hold that all effort involving methods and practices for opening to realization are useless and are in themselves fixations and distractions, since they suggest a distance between "us" and "enlightenment," whereas there is no distance at all — everything is already complete. More fundamentally, the direct path contends there is no "us" and no "enlightenment" — these are simply thoughts representing the illusory dualism of subject and object.

I don't believe we need to take sides in these controversies. My own sense is that, except for their insistence on being the one correct view, both sides are accurate in their own context.

In my experience, this work is both gradual *and* direct. The Open Path of nonduality we are exploring here is a gradual path to the extent it is a path of unlearning. It is a direct path because it also acknowledges that clear awareness is already present and complete, and thus no effort and no "doing" is required to realize it. As an early Tibetan tantra points out: Once we are *free of old habits and ambitions...enlightened intent is spontaneously present by nature. Nothing need be done about what has always been so.*

We may be able to sense within our own experience how these paradoxical views regarding effort and no effort, practice and no practice, are resolved simply by the attitude with which we embrace this work. If we are full of effortful practicing we are clearly divided from what we yearn for; however, if we are seduced by the laxity of effortlessness and non-practice we are at risk of dispersion. Approaching this work with an appropriate attitude may release us from settling into either of these extremes.

In a beautiful passage in Sri Nisargadatta's book *I Am That,* he responds to a questioner who asks about the appropriate "mood" for inquiry. Nisargadatta responds, *You must be serious, intent, truly interested. You must be full of goodwill for yourself!* And in another passage he says:

> If you are earnest, whatever way you choose will take you to your goal. It is the earnestness that is the decisive factor. Earnestness is the homing instinct, which makes the bird re-

turn to its nest and the fish to the mountain stream where it was born. The seed returns to the earth, when the fruit is ripe.

Nurturing an attitude of earnestness and goodwill for oneself is fundamentally different from being motivated by a gaining idea. It is a matter of being coherent, not divided against your wholeness. The Sufi teacher Inayat Khan, when asked about the attitude that is most essential for those who wish initiation, responded, "It is sincerity." This is the same quality as earnestness. One dedicates oneself to realization as "sincerely" as a mother cares for her child, or a flower opens to the sunlight.

LONGING AND FINDING

As I mentioned earlier, the cultivation of spiritual longing may be a detour, in the sense that it may keep us entranced in a subject-object relationship with that which we long for, whether we call this longed-for one "the Beloved," "the Truth," or "open awareness." And yet, as we have seen, the other side of this dilemma shows us that if we do not dedicate ourselves thoroughly, we may easily be lost in distraction.

The arrow will never reach the target if the bowstring is not drawn back with sufficient one-pointed intensity. At the same time, if the archer draws back the bowstring but never lets go, never releases its longing, the arrow goes nowhere.

You might not regard your motivation for doing this work as "longing." Even so, you may be able to appreciate the dynamic represented by the word, in that it signifies a quality of whole-heartedness and reverence toward what is longed for. For those of you who are comfortable with the word and experience of longing, it is helpful to remember that at a certain point *longing must free itself from itself.* It must "self-liberate."

Here again, Jelaluddin Rumi may be our best guide. He says of
longing:

> *Longing is the core of mystery.*
> *Longing itself is the cure.*
> *The only rule is: Suffer the pain.*
>
> *Your desire must be disciplined,*
> *and what you want to happen*
> *in time, sacrificed.*[20]

What you want to happen in time — this is our longing, our hope
for realization, which when disciplined becomes its own cure: it transcends itself.

I am describing all of this not because I think it is an interesting
subject, but because it is an unavoidable challenge on the open path
we are traveling. Our motivation for realization, our longing for
union with the divine, and our attitude of sincerity, all support us
in the not-always-easy work of *unlearning*: observing, inquiring into,
and deconstructing fixations and habits of mind and emotion. But
when that work is familiar and happens as a matter of course, the
only move left is to let go of all ideas of "moves," all effort, motivation, seeking, longing for anything, or of having an appropriate attitude. In the words of Jean Klein:

> You must leave behind the idea of improving. There is nothing
> to be found, nothing to achieve. Searching and wanting to
> achieve something are the fuel for the entity you believe your-
> self to be. Don't project an idea of reality, of freedom. Be sim-
> ply aware of the facts of your existence without wanting to
> change. Seeing things in this way will bring you a state of deep
> relaxation both physical and psychological...

Any form of exercise is bound to a goal, to a result. But this is an obstacle when there is no goal to be reached since what you are looking for is here now and always has been. When the mind is free of all desire to become, it is at peace....Be vigilant, clear-sighted, aware of your constant desire to be this or that and don't make any effort. What you are is without direction so all direction takes you away from knowingly being what you are.

EFFORTLESSNESS

In human terms, we say something "takes effort" because we experience our body or mind expending energy. We say it takes effort to build a house or to give birth to a baby or ride a bicycle. Because we identify with the body and the mind, we infer that "we" somehow supply that energy and effort. Is this really the case? Where does the energy come from? From our effort? What actually *is* effort? Is it *willing*? Is it *trying*? Is it *struggling*? It seems our idea of "putting effort into something" is a way of asserting that we are the source of the energy that makes things happen. Is this so? Look carefully, for example, at the effort you may feel you are putting into reading and understanding this sentence. Where does it start, or come from? You? How does that happen?

Contemplate the sun for a moment, this enormous outpouring of stellar energy that has occurred for billions of years now and that will continue for billions more. Does it take effort for the sun to do this? Or watch how the wind moves tree branches, or how the current of a river flows. Does it take effort for the wind to move the branches, or for the river to flow? Obviously not, these natural processes happen effortlessly. Rain falls effortlessly, plants grow effortlessly, light shines effortlessly.

What would it be like for me to live my life effortlessly? Not, of course, without expending energy — this happens with every blink and movement I make — but without feeling as if I had to exert effort — to struggle — to make things happen, or that I have to somehow lean into each action to make it occur. The operative word here is "I:" I have to apply effort, I have to struggle, I have to lean into an action.

Living effortlessly, first of all, means abandoning the belief that I am an independent entity who makes things happen through some kind of deliberate, original force that I apply, namely *will*. All it takes to release this belief is to investigate, first hand, how action actually happens, and how effort emanates from us, if it does. This investigation parallels our explorations in chapter three into the nature of volition. In the exercises at the end of this chapter you will find some further suggestions for investigating the nature of effort and effortlessness. Here we are bringing our inquiry, once again, to look directly into the nature of the self and its claim of agency.

But even if we accept intellectually that we are not independent entities with independent agency, this doesn't magically bring us into a life of effortlessness. Living effortlessly — as Rumi describes it: like "an eagle gliding out from the face of a cliff" — also means living without resistance, and without worries or complaints, which are expressions of resistance. When we do something with effort — for example, finishing our taxes, or painting a ceiling, or changing a flat tire — the "effort" or struggle we experience is largely about overcoming our resistance to doing the task.

Let's imagine how this might play out with the example of a flat tire. Resistance: *Oh I have a flat tire — I hate that! Now I have to get out of my quiet car, endure the blasts of wind from traffic, rummage through the trunk, find the jack and spare tire, unscrew the wheel nuts, wrestle the flat off and the spare on, oh God! This is awful! I hate it! What an effort!* The energy required to change the tire proceeds, but each step is encased in complaint and self-pity. One feels enormous effort is required to do each step, effort that is actually expended in pushing through all the self-generated resistance to the situation.

A scenario of no resistance to the flat tire would be markedly different, although there wouldn't be much commentary, except maybe: *Oh, a flat tire. Better pull off. Here's a place. Where's the spare? Oh yeah, under the trunk. Gotta move that stuff to the back seat. Mmmm, how does this jack fit into the stand? Oh yeah, this way. Let's see, where does this fit? Oh yeah...* etc. No resistance simply means accepting what is, moment by moment. When you face not being sure how the jack fits into its stand, you accept that without needing to complain, and then go from there: *Let's see, this way? No. Maybe this way? Ah, that part fits in that thing.* Problem solving is much more possible because you're not spending energy on resisting the situation. This is not making a problem out of a problem.

Not making a problem out of a problem applies in every situation — if you don't have a spare tire, or if you can't physically lift the tire, or turn the wheel nuts, then you accept that and go from there. Responding to what is without conditioning the next moment with our discomfort for this one frees us from a life of efforting, struggle, and distaste.

This may sound reasonable, but in the nitty-gritty of the moment when you are resisting doing something, how can you break free of this reaction? Here we return to the Open Path dynamics of motivation (good will toward yourself and all beings), sincerity, observing what is actually happening, noticing the nature of the resistance — how it sounds and feels, noticing the imagined entity of your self taking a position of judgment, looking directly into who or what this entity is that seems to be taking a position or is threatened by the situation, etc.

As we have seen earlier, noticing in these ways brings us face to face with the realization that everything that occurs is spontaneously released — unless we keep generating a point of view about what's happening. Generating a point of view — that is, resistance — loses its traction the moment we notice what's happening. So our only "job" is to notice what is.

Does it take effort to notice what is? I don't think so. Noticing what is is the natural function of awareness. Since awareness is freely given, no effort is required!

As I mentioned above, gradually all of this noticing and releasing becomes intimately familiar to us and happens as a matter of course. When disturbances occur in our life, as they most assuredly will, we free ourselves from consternation about them in these ways, and then simply respond to them without effort, without fuss, as appropriately as we can.

In the end, effortlessness is selflessness. Not considering ourselves an entity who needs to struggle to make our way in life, we live as openness and spontaneous presence.

We will return to the subject of effortlessness and nonaction in chapter nine.

CONCLUSION

In this chapter we reflected on the delicate nature of our engagement with "path" and "goal," and the spirit that calls us to this work. We recognized the hook of a gaining idea that can be hidden in our motivation for awakening, and how the most natural motivation for awakening is simply *because we have to* — for the wellbeing of all.

We also recognized that the methods and practices of any spiritual path, the Open Path included, can easily make a conceptual nest in our minds, and in that nest we can try to situate ourselves and become comfortable. But the essence of this work is not about building nests. Through repeated experiential release we gradually discover a natural ease of being that frees us from the need to come to conclusions — or to hold onto anything — including any self-concept, or hope.

Finally, we began to explore the nature of effortlessness, and how it leads to releasing the idea of individual agency and of resistance to what is. Here we sense again the very openness of the Open Path: in all the observation of fixations, in all the letting go of identifications, in all our reading and talking about these subjects, and in our self-inquiry, the most important thing is to allow space, to allow ourselves to be what we naturally are: effortlessly at ease.

Exercises: Motivation and Effortlessness

Motivation and Attitude

Write your responses, or share them with a close friend or practice partner, to the following questions:

1   What is it you most want to occur through your study and practice of the Open Path?

2   Describe your motivation for doing this work, especially: what brings you back to it when you feel tired of it, or out of touch with it, or in disagreement with some aspect of the teaching, or disappointed with your own experience of it?

3   Describe the spirit or attitude in which you engage in the practice of subtle opening and the other methods of noticing fixations and self-inquiry we have explored so far. Would you describe your attitude as "full of goodwill for yourself?" Would you describe it as wholly sincere? If not, can you say anything about the lack of sincerity or goodwill in your attitude?

Effortlessness

Over the next few days, on your own, investigate the difference between doing something with, and without, effort or struggle. For example, when you climb a flight of stairs, or a hill, explore how you might do this by exerting effort, and then effortlessly. What in your experience actually constitutes effort?

Notice also the many things you do effortlessly, like remembering something, or laughing, or gesturing with your hands while you speak, or having a conversation. Experiment by doing any of these things with effort. For example, explore what is added when you try hard (with effort) to remember something, and when you do so effortlessly?

Did it take effort for you to read this chapter? If it did, describe what exactly it "took." Does it take effort to answer this question?

What role does overcoming resistance play in your doing something with effort? What about overcoming worry? Or overcoming complaining?

Lastly, identify something that you normally do with effort — perhaps washing a burned saucepan, or ironing a pile of shirts, or scraping ice off your car's windshield — and explore doing this effortlessly, even for a few moments.

The River Flow Meditation

Up to this time, I hope you have been able to explore on a regular basis *the Practice of Subtle Opening* introduced in chapter two. The meditation described here — *the River Flow Meditation* — offers a slightly different way for you to engage with the third part of the Practice of Subtle Opening. As you will recall, the instruction for the third part is simply: "do nothing." As you will see, you can incorporate this river flow practice into the subtle opening practice without much change.

The River Flow Meditation is an adaptation I've made of a Buddhist practice suggested by the Dzogchen translator and teacher Keith Dowman. Its function is to create a metaphorical image that can serve to integrate several aspects of our work in a direct, experiential way. Here are the instructions:

> Sitting calmly in a relaxed yet awake way, with your eyes
> closed, imagine a great wide river. In the middle of the river is

a small uninhabited island, and you are on that island. You walk to the upstream end of the island and see a wide, flat, moss-covered rock at the very upstream tip of the island. You step onto it and sit down, looking upstream.

Now your field of vision is completely of the river flowing toward you. You notice the flashes of sunlight on the water, little waves appearing and disappearing, and various things floating down the river. Whatever you see appears for a moment or two, and then passes on downstream in the river's current.

Now just sit there doing nothing. Allow whatever appears in your awareness — thoughts, sensations, emotions — to be like branches, leaves, and foam floating by in the river. They appear for a moment or two, but you don't do anything with them, you don't try to catch them, or inspect them, or even name them. You just let them appear as they do, and then vanish, as they do.

Just relax in the "first moment" of whatever is appearing in the river of your awareness. If you find you have become involved in a thought or emotion, notice that involvement too is simply something floating past, and don't do anything about it. Let it go. The river takes it away naturally. There is nothing for you to do.

Whenever you feel your attention drawn away by the fascinating things in the current, simply return to the first moment in which new images, shapes, thoughts, or feelings appear. Just be with their appearing. Notice that this "returning" to the first moment is not really a "doing" — it's where awareness is naturally.

Hold onto nothing. Do nothing.

· 7 ·

ON NONDUALITY
AND PRAYER

Our exploration of the Open Path up to this point has been focused on recognizing the thoughts, beliefs, and emotional habits that fuel both the discomforts and ambitions of our life, and that prop up our belief that we are a separate self. We have been learning to release our attachments to these beliefs and thoughts, one by one, again and again, gently, without aggression, with the purpose of opening our awareness into its seamless unity with the transparent presence of timeless being.

While we use phrases like "the transparent presence of timeless being" and "open awareness," we continually remind ourselves that these labels do not refer to any thing. No transcendent object or entity or God is being named. Indeed, a large part of our work is to discover and release our habitual tendency of reifying (objectifying) any spiritual goal or ideal in our present experience.

Many people point out that such a nondual discipline or view seems to be in conflict with traditional approaches to spirituality.

Subject-object, human-divine, samsara-nirvana polarities are empha-
sized throughout the great majority of the world's spiritual traditions.
Sufism, for example, in its essence is grounded in nondual
realization — *wahdat al wujud* — "the Oneness of Being." However,
many Sufi writings and teachings could be interpreted as intensifying
theism rather than pointing to a path beyond it. Much Islamic Sufi
writing is an affirmation of the One True God and His Prophet, describing in great detail the criteria for a proper human relationship to
God. My own root lineage — the Western universal Sufism introduced by Pir-o-Murshid Inayat Khan — while not exclusively tied to
Islam or any other religion — can be seen as often emphasizing theism, especially in the language of many of the prayers and aphorisms.

Indeed, most forms of theistic and prayerful language are typically
experienced as descriptions of subject and object relationships. When
Christians pray *Our Father who art in heaven, hallowed be Thy Name,*
the Father is sensed as an entity somehow separate from us, to whom
we address our prayers. This kind of implicit dualism in religious
expression is familiar to us, and is often pointed to as one reason
why so many people have become disaffected with religion in modern times.

But prayer is not simply a formal religious expression. Even those
of us who do not pray nevertheless participate in prayerful attitudes.
We may wish that friends who die "find peace" or "rest in peace," or
that the suffering of the world may be lessened or that "all beings
may be happy." These are prayers. Even if they are not addressed to
God they are offered up to the universal presence we share. They express our sincere wishes for harmony and wellbeing. Even common
expressions such as "happy birthday" or "have a good day" or raising
our glasses in a toast carry a certain quality of prayer. The implicit
dualism of prayer using "God language" is less evident in these everyday examples, but still can be sensed in the very function of "making
a wish." We want to positively affect the future with our words of
invocation. We take a position, a point of reference — we are an "I"

who seeks to affect an outcome by wishing for it to be so. The polarity of subject and object is an essential part of this kind of wishing or praying.

So we have a dilemma: if our aim is to release the conceit of being a separate self and open our awareness to what is and has always been true — the nondual unity of original nature — then doesn't the act of praying reinforce the idea of duality rather than release it? Through prayer are we not imposing a duality between the one who prays and the One prayed to? No matter how sweet it may make us feel, praying runs the risk of reifying the Unnamable into an object, *causing* us to be separate from our "Beloved," to use a favorite Sufi word.

In this chapter we will explore this seeming dilemma as carefully as we can, for doing so may help align us with, and benefit from, the practice of prayer — or prayerful intention — as we engage with the work of the Open Path.

I am not suggesting that you should develop an active prayer life if you do not already have one. Recognizing pure, open, contentless awareness does not depend on prayer or belief in God. Nevertheless, many of us do pray — or at least we invoke good outcomes for others and ourselves. Can prayer in any of its forms serve our larger intention here?

My view is that prayer *can* be engaged in ways that deepen our sincerity and our capacity to open to unconditioned awareness, rather than obstruct it. However, this is best accomplished with a clear recognition of the limits of prayer and the detours and dead-ends it may present. I will consider here both some of the gifts and the limits of prayer, and suggest ways to pray that may serve the process of liberation, rather than undermine it.

TO BEGIN AT THE END

It may help put our contemplations on prayer into a clear perspective if we consider for a moment the place of prayer, if any, for the one who has opened into the spontaneous presence of timeless awareness. Does prayer have a function from the identityless and positionless perspective of nondual awakening? Probably not, except as a kind of celebration of love and gratitude. The need for prayer ceases when we remember the open transparent awareness we are, not different from the awakeness of everything. There is no need to use prayer instrumentally to ask that things be different than they are. The same understanding is held by Sufis about *zikr* (the repetition of sacred words; literally, "remembering"): at the most realized levels of *zikr,* the *zikr* ceases. One remembers, and the need for reminding ends.

Nevertheless, there are stories of realized sages who continue to chant their hymns and repeat their *manis* on prayer beads, even though they are purely awakened. Asked why, they say *"Because I am happy to do it."* This is prayer that is not instrumental but more like a song. We will explore both the instrumental and noninstrumental aspects of prayer in what follows.

STARTING WHERE WE ARE

Each of us represents the leading edge of an evolving life-form that has been shaped by countless conditions. These conditions have resulted in the body we have right now, the language we speak, the traumas and suffering we endure, the beauty we share, and our thoughts, feelings, hopes and fears. We are embedded in conditionality. As long as our view of reality is limited to conditionality we obviously experience the logic of duality — of subject-object, good-bad, like-don't like, before-after, etc. The great majority of human beings never glimpse beyond this logic, at least until the death of the body.

Prayer, being largely dualistic in its syntax, simply *starts from the same place we are.* Prayer's duality reflects our own experience of duality. We experience ourselves as separate beings, separate from each other, separate from the earth, and separate from what we conceive of as God or the transcendent. Prayer — in many of its forms — acknowledges this sense of separation while it gathers us into itself exactly because we are suffering from the illusion of separation. It is naturally compassionate in this way. Although the sense of being a separate self must one day vanish, prayer welcomes that sense into its formulations, and then works to make the self's seeming solidity and importance less dominant in our consciousness.

Nondual approaches to awakening often employ methods that cause a direct confrontation with our habitual manner of thinking and experiencing life. Direct approaches like *koans* and self-inquiry can have the effect of jolting us out of these habits. But they also can have no effect at all, simply seeming odd, or contradictory. If these approaches to nondual realization are a ladder to climb out of the hole we are trapped in, the first rung of the ladder may often be experienced as too high to reach.

Prayer can serve as another rung on the ladder, an easier reach (even though the ladder is a fiction, as is the climber). Or we might think of prayer as a bridge that is accessible to us in our seeming condition of distance, confusion, and longing. It provides a sense of direction, a *towardness* — *Toward the One* as the Sufi prayer begins — a flowing, a promise of reconnection. In this way we hear the prayers of our ancestors, we repeat them, and we feel a lift from the great chorus of souls who also have stepped onto that bridge.

PRAYERS OF PETITION

In most people's minds, prayer is synonymous with asking for something. It is petition and supplication. While there are many other types of prayer — prayers of praise, gratitude, invocation, confession, blessing, celebration, etc. — we often find prayer to be a calling for some benefit, that is, instrumental prayer. Even in the context of this chapter and our work together, we can notice this instrumental tendency at work: e.g., I am inviting us to see prayer as a method for (1) preparing us for awakening, and (2) initiating the release into selflessness. We want something to profoundly change in our lives and this kind of prayer expresses that.

This is fine — although it definitely carries some dangers for our journey (non-journey) of awakening into what is already here, the spontaneous presence of open awareness. We will consider these dangers later. For now, let us note that prayers of petition carry the fundamental benefit of stirring our deepest longing for the divine, as well as of freeing us from attachment to the inessential in our lives. A spiritual integration happens when we pray sincerely. Our experience as a human being becomes less fragmented. The sincerity of our prayers, the love they express, is light in itself — as we hear in this poem of Rumi:

> One night a man was crying,
>   Allah! Allah!
> His lips grew sweet with the praising,
> until a cynic said,
>   "So! I have heard you
> calling out, but have you ever
> gotten any response?"
>
> The man had no answer to that.
> He quit praying and fell into a confused sleep.
>
> He dreamed he saw Khidr, the guide of souls,
> in a thick, green foliage.
>   "Why did you stop praising?"
> "Because I never heard anything back."

"This longing
you express is the return message."

The grief you cry out from
draws you toward union.

Your pure sadness
that wants help
is the secret cup.

Listen to the moan of a dog for its master.
That whining is the connection.

There are love dogs
no one knows the names of.

Give your life to be one of them.[21]

INDIRECT BENEFITS OF A PRAYERFUL LIFE

Apart from the blessings directly petitioned for in prayer, and the gift of spiritual integration and love-connection mentioned above, other benefits of a more indirect nature arise in a prayerful life. It is as if by returning to the place of prayer, our experience is opened, purified, and made resonant with levels of energy that may not appear to our conscious minds. Imagine, for example, the effect on a Tibetan Buddhist or a Moroccan Muslim who each day prostrates his body in prayers to his conception or anticipation of the divine. It's not hard to imagine what the long-term effects of such prayer might be: an increased humility and capacity for surrender, and perhaps an accompanying ease and openness of heart.

There are three basic modes of prayer: *invocatory prayer* (as in *zikr* and mantra), *spontaneous prayer* (personal and unique), and *liturgical prayer* (traditional written prayers). Each mode yields benefits in the prayerful heart.

Invocatory prayer helps to purify and center one's attention and reduce the speed and volume of stray thoughts, emotions, and images. It calms us. Repeating the name *Allah* five thousand times each day can have this effect; it can also deepen our capacity for reverence. Long repetitions of the "Name" or other sacred formulas (*Om mani padme hung*) may also function on neuro-physiological levels, freeing neural pathways that may have become dysfunctional through long-established habits of anxious thinking or other fixations. This is experienced as purification.

Spontaneous prayer of the heart offers different benefits. One quality that arises from spontaneous prayer is a more intimate kind of centering than that experienced through invocation. When you sit on a hill under the stars and pray spontaneously for guidance or opening or forgiveness, the sincerity of your prayer brings you to a centered, intimate, face-to-face dimension with the reality to which you address your prayer. In fact it is the face-to-face aspect that forces your sincerity — if your lips are next to God's ear, how sincerely you speak! Spontaneous prayer is a cure for insincerity.

Liturgical prayer may nourish many qualities — reverence, humility, awe, faith, gratitude, forgiveness, humane-ness, praise. Of course invocatory and spontaneous prayer can nourish these same qualities; however, the vast treasury of liturgical prayer from the world's religions has survived precisely because it is helpful in opening these qualities in us. Read again this well-loved prayer:

> *The Lord is my Shepherd; I shall not want.*
> *He maketh me to lie down in green pastures:*
> *He leadeth me beside still waters,*

He restoreth my soul:
He leadeth me in the paths of righteousness for His name's sake.

Yea, though I walk through the valley of the shadow of death,
I will fear no evil: For Thou art with me;
Thy rod and Thy staff, they comfort me.
Thou preparest a table before me in the presence of my enemies;
Thou annointest my head with oil; My cup runneth over.

Surely goodness and mercy shall follow me all the days of my life,
And I will dwell in the House of the Lord forever. (Psalm 23)

Consider the effect of repeating this prayer sincerely each night before sleep. Its images and the calm certainty of its voice resonate in us, nurturing acceptance and faith in our hearts. As well, there is the image of the Lord as shepherd, care-giver, protector, and guide. Although this is an image and an idealization, and therefore dualistic and conditional, it nevertheless stimulates both anticipation of a presence beyond our conception and the release of our sense of self-importance.

At its best, sincere prayer reaches beyond itself toward the non-conceptual perception of reality. The Lord, the Shepherd, the Hallowed Name — these names are signifiers for what is beyond them: the Nameless and the infinite generosity that emanates from Namelessness. By naming them and holding them as the object of our prayers, we create a space in ourselves, a capacity of heart and mind, an *akasha* (potential) for the presence of the Unspeakable and Unnamable to be intuited. Of course, each of us already *is* that capacity and akasha, and there is actually no space that needs to be created — nevertheless, authentic prayer has the capacity to simulate conditions in us that — as Ibn al 'Arabi said — "put you in the way of grace." Like meditation, prayer is not necessary for awakening, but it sets up conditions that can make the spontaneous intimation of our natural state more likely.

I have mentioned a number of these conditions already — qualities such as centeredness, sincerity, humility, reverence, awe, faith, and gratitude. By deepening our capacity to live these qualities, prayer serves to make the "boundary" between self-identification and identitylessness more porous.

PRAYERS OF APPROACH AND NEARNESS

One function of prayer is to create a kind of spatial and temporal expectation. It heralds, alerts, announces, invokes, as well as leads, guides, and brings us close. For example, many prayers begin with an invocation:

> Bismillah!
> Toward the One!
> Om Nama Shivaya!
> O Great Spirit
> Whose voice I hear in the winds,
> and whose breath gives life to all the world,
> hear me!

The effect of these invocatory prayers is to signal it is now time to align ourselves *as if* we are actually approaching God and God is approaching us. Their purpose is to *get us to look up* from our everyday preoccupations, to sense the majesty of what we are involved in here. This creates an inner condition of opening and anticipation, a readiness, as in this beautiful prayer-song from Taizé:

> *Wait for the Lord, His day is near,*
> *Wait for the Lord, keep watch, take heart.*

Approach brings us near, and nearness is intimacy. "God" and the "Lord" become "Beloved" and the "Friend" in Sufi poetry. By addressing the unimaginable Real as "Thee" or "Thou" we make a quasi-imaginable entity to which we can draw near. *To make God intelligible you must make a God of your own. (Inayat Khan)*

Sufis are well known for their beautiful love words to God. Perhaps this originated from the tradition of classical Arabic odes (*qasidas*) that typically began with remembrances of the lost beloved. This love-yearning easily merged with the longing of the mystic, and over the centuries Sufis included in their prayers, songs, and poetry the associated themes of love-madness, divine intoxication, perpetual wandering, and the tantalizing nearness of the Beloved.

"Nearness of the Beloved" is best experienced rather than read about. We read words about it like this poem of Hafiz, but the joy and helplessness it refers to can be known only when it is happening within us.

My heart sits on the Arm of God
Like a tethered falcon
Suddenly unhooded.

I am now blessedly crazed
Because my Master's Astounding Effulgence
Is in constant view.

My piercing eyes,
Which have searched every world
For Tenderness and Love,
Now lock on the Royal Target —
The Wild Holy One
Whose Beauty Illuminates Existence.

My soul endures a magnificent longing.

I am a tethered falcon
With great wings and sharp talons poised,
Every sinew taut, like a Sacred Bow,
Quivering at the edge of my Self
And Eternal Freedom,

Though still held in check
By a miraculous
Divine Golden Cord.

Beloved,
I am waiting for You to free me
Into Your Mind
And Infinite Being.
I am pleading in absolute helplessness
To hear, finally, your Words of Grace:
"Fly! Fly into Me!"

Hafiz,
Who can understand
Your sublime Nearness and Separation?[22]

THE LIMITS OF PRAYER

We have been surveying very briefly the lift prayer can give us in opening our hearts and minds. To summarize, prayer:

- starts from where we are (compassionate access to the journey)
- gives a sense of direction and therefore possible release
- focuses the deepest desire of our heart

- frees us from the nonessential
- integrates a sense of self, so we may be better able to release that sense
- centers and calms the mind (invocatory prayer)
- deepens our sincerity
- nourishes qualities such as reverence, humility, awe, faith, and gratitude
- helps to reduce self-preoccupation
- creates a "space" in us, an *akasha*, a capacity of heart and mind for the unknown
- stimulates an anticipation and readiness for the extra-ordinary
- opens us to "intimacy-with" rather than "knowing-about" that which is called God

And yet there are limits to these benefits, and in many ways the lift they provide can turn into a weight and burden. Perhaps the most obvious danger comes from imagining that God is an entity, and then relating that entity to what we think of as our own entity-ness. It is not surprising that we picture our religious cosmologies in this way. The notion of my self as something that takes up space and exists in time, and the image of a God that does the same, arise from the customary view of our conditioned minds; it is how we expect things to be. Hence we have ideas such as "approach" and "nearness," of a journey to God and the expectation that awakening is an event that happens in time.

From the nondual perspective, the ideas of approach and nearness are irrelevant. From this view any grammar that imagines a distance between "us" and "God" makes a conceptual arrangement out of a reality that cannot be conceived. The idea that there are entities called "we," an entity called "God," and a "space" between them, while it may have some initial utility, is like a cane one cannot part with after the leg is healed. As Inayat Khan reminds us, *The ideal is the means, but its breaking is the goal.* The human tendency is to grasp the conceptual ideal itself and refuse to let it go.

Even nearness, the idea so dear to Sufis, has meaning only as the description of a relationship between two separate entities. No matter how much consolation God's proximity makes us feel, within the logic of nearness there can never be a meeting.

Prayers that emphasize a theistic entity can perpetuate a dualistic worldview in other ways as well. They can reinforce the idea that we are self-willed and sovereign beings; that God judges "souls" and somehow consigns these seemingly permanent entities to existences in heaven or hell; that "individuals" are to "blame" for certain transgressions; or that the earth is corrupt but God's kingdom is elsewhere and pure. Most of us have experienced these kinds of dualistic and judgmental concepts expressed in traditional religions. It is not difficult to see how they have done immense harm to the potential for happiness and for enlightened human society.

LEARNING TO PRAY WISELY

Acknowledging these pitfalls on the path of a prayerful life, is there any way for us to pray whole-heartedly, to be uplifted by the blessings of prayer without being weighed down by dualism?

I would answer these questions with a qualified "yes." If we are to joyfully embrace prayer as a support for preparing us — "anointing our heads with oil," so to speak — as we open to clear timeless awareness, then we must become ever more sensitive to the tendencies of dualistic language in prayers. The Open Path, as I understand it, is inclusive. This means, among other things, that we can embrace prayer as easily as we might embrace any other compassionate and effective support for our awakening.

To do this we must learn to be good translators, freeing dualistic language into nondual recognition. Thus in our hearts the word *God* might equal something like *radiantly open and spontaneously present awareness* — not specifically those words, but the clear spaciousness behind them. Becoming good translators is not just a matter of shifting words to our liking. It is about releasing our judgments of their limitations into the essence they hope to signify.

A life of prayer can prepare us, break us open, and reduce our self-importance to dust. It can scoop out our small, preconceived thoughts about what is true, and humble us before the unknown. Allowing the power of prayer to strike us in this way can be extremely powerful. For this to happen, we must be poets of prayer, continually translating and freeing their messages from the words that enclose them.

> *Lo, I am with you always means when you look for God,*
> *God is in the look of your eyes,*
> *in the thought of looking, nearer to you than yourself,*
> *or things that have happened to you.*
> *There's no need to go outside.*
>
> *Be melting snow.*
> *Wash yourself of yourself.*[23]
>
> —*Rumi*

PRAYERS OF IDENTITY

As we mature in a life of prayer we eventually come to the middle of the bridge — the bridge that prayer creates to carry us to the "other shore." But suddenly we see ahead that the bridge has disappeared! And as we take the next steps we notice that we too begin to disappear! We are vanishing! This is the experience described in prayers of *identity*. Prayers of identity are different from prayers that nurture the approach and nearness to God in that they explicitly seek to deconstruct their dualistic language to reveal unity.

The beautiful prayer of Ibn al 'Arabi — *Take me away from myself and be my being, then shall You see everything through my eyes* — is a prayer of identity. As one prays this prayer sincerely, the edges of one's self are made porous and permeable. In fact, removing the imaginary distinction between God and self is the actual subject of the prayer — *take this away!* Dualistic language and doctrine become instruments for their own dissolving.

In this regard, prayers of identity have the same power as *koans*, or self-inquiry, or the poetry of Rumi, Hafiz, and other mystics. Contradiction built into their grammar and their meaning twists our normal ways of comprehension. If we are to open to the power of these prayers, we must be willing to let go of what we think we know.

To illustrate, let us consider this beautiful "prayer of identity" from Inayat Khan:

> *Thy light hath illuminated the dark chambers of my mind;*
> *Thy love is rooted in the depths of my heart;*
> *Thine own eyes are the light of my soul;*
> *Thy power worketh behind my action;*
> *Thy will is behind my every impulse;*
> *Thy voice is audible in the words I speak;*
> *Thine own image is my countenance.*
> *My body is but a cover over Thy soul;*
> *my life is Thy very breath, my Beloved,*
> *and my self is Thine own being.*[24]

Each line of this prayer gently breaks through the polarization of *I-Thou,* even though there is continual reference to "Thy" and

"Thine." The impact of the prayer is a deconstruction of the sub-ject-object fixation, revealing the identity of the one who prays as that which is prayed "to."

Thy light hath illuminated the dark chambers of my mind —

This first line is the only line of the prayer set in the past tense. It says: this has happened, it is so, the dark chambers of my mind have been illuminated, and in this illumination I see:

Thy love is rooted in the depths of my heart —

My heart, my most private and personally unique realm, is rec-ognized as being not actually mine. Neither is the love that is rooted there mine. Its origin is not from me. My innermost realm is Thy love. Then what does "my" and "mine" mean? Where are the edges of my self?

Thine own eyes are the light of my soul —

This line moves even deeper. The very light by which I know my "soul" or my existence, the light of my being or "am-ness," is how the Nameless One (Thou) sees and is awake.

Thy power worketh behind my action —

Could this be? These actions of mine, these movements of my body, each smile or laugh or shout, each word and work — where does the power that drives them come from? Is it not "my" power? If it is "Thine" then are these actions "mine" at all?

Thy will is behind my every impulse —

Any distinction between my life and "Thy" life ceases with this line. My every impulse! Who is in charge here? Where do these im-pulses come from? If each impulse is Thy will then I give up! Who gives up? Who ever had anything to give up?

Thy voice is audible in the words I speak —

Each remaining line of this prayer draws closer the intimate real-ization. The province of "me" loses all sovereignty. These words! Where do they come from? *Who speaks these words with my mouth?* Thy voice is audible, even now. Who is speaking?

Thine own image is my countenance —

My countenance? My face is my countenance, but not as I perceive it in a mirror, rather it is my countenance as I perceive it from
the inside. I perceive it not as an image but as an openness, an absence of image. This absence of image is "Thine own image."

My body is but a cover over Thy soul —

My body is a cover not over "my" soul but Thine! Who is here?
What am I?

My life is Thy very breath, my Beloved —

A feather on the breath of God...or even subtler...I am being
breathed, not even I — Rumi says — but this *breath breathing
human being.*

and my self is Thine own being —

Here I reach the other shore, bridge disappeared, and no one has
reached anything. Only "Thine own being" remains, although without "I" there is no "Thee." Only Identity. Only This, which has
never been hidden.

Our prayer releases us beyond prayer, where there is no longer the
idea of separation.

PRAYERS OF SILENCE

Finally, let us consider the most subtle form of prayer: silence, and
the radiant life it gives birth to. My Sufi teacher Murshid Fazal Inayat-Khan once said, "Praying with words is good, but one day we
must learn to pray without words." Praying without words — these
are the prayers of silence: pure openness, responsiveness, transparency, life pouring forth.

Prayers of silence, unlike prayers with words, are not instrumental.
They don't ask for anything or look for an effect. They don't prepare
us for union — they arise from it, silent at their core and radiant in
the life they express. Lived in this way, our life becomes a prayer
without words. We pray without ceasing. We play. A natural joy and

compassion arises in the living of life, along with an innocent curiosity, silent at its heart, outwardly a song.

These words of Inayat Khan about belief in God can also apply to this contemplation of the living quality of prayer:

> Happiness cannot come by merely believing in God. Believing is a process. By this process the God within is awakened and made living; it is the living in God which gives happiness.
>
> The deepest prayer is a process in which awareness of God Within and being Within God is awakened. It is awakened in a living silence that permeates all.

Exercises: On Nonduality and Prayer

The following exercises are offered to those of you who wish to explore aspects of prayer more experientially. Some of you may already have an active prayer life, and these exercises may or may not be relevant for you. Others may have no interest in exploring prayer further. There is no problem either way. However, for those of you who are drawn to prayer, these exercises may offer some experiences that will serve to deepen your prayer life, and open qualities of prayer that support awakening to our natural state.

1   Invocatory Prayer. You have already experienced one style of invocatory prayer in the *practice of subtle opening*, particularly in the repetition of *Ya Latif*. You may wish to explore repeating other prayers in this way. At this point, to keep things simple, I suggest you choose one of the following words to use as your zikr: *Ya Qayyum* (the Self-Sustaining One), *Ya Hayy* (the Alive), or *Hallelujiah*. Begin by sitting quietly in a good space, with your back upright — feeling both alert and relaxed. You can do these invocations in one of two ways: (1) repeat the word aloud at a comfortable rate, about once per second or so; you may wish to use prayer beads — they help keep you steady; try to do at least one thousand repetitions or for about fifteen minutes, and then extend this amount gradually as you feel ready, up to three thousand repetitions each day; these repetitions may slowly

shift from being pronounced aloud to repeating them silently, at the same rate or even faster; or (2) repeat the word silently on your breath — once on the in-breath and once on the out-breath; since this is slower, you may wish to begin repeating this breath-prayer for about fifteen minutes and then increase the time as you feel ready.

2   Spontaneous Prayer. Find a place where you can be alone — in nature is best. Address God, the four directions, spirit, or the universe — say who you are and why you are praying: to express your heart's deepest desire. This may be one thing, it may be several. Your prayer can be said either aloud or silently; aloud may not be as easy but can give an added depth to your prayer — you may wish to whisper. When you are finished, thank whatever you have addressed your prayer to and make a gesture of respect, such as a bow or placing your hand over your heart.

3   Using the following prayer from Inayat Khan — recite it over several days at different times. Become aware of its effect, and perhaps how your mind may approve or disapprove of different words or lines in it. Explore "translating" whatever dualistic expressions you experience in the prayer into a nondual spirit, not necessarily making up new words (although you can do that too), but simply seeing through them so their subject-object quality may relax into their nondual source. For example, the word "Thou" could be seen with a sense of its inclusion of all.

> *Oh Thou, the perfection of love, harmony and beauty,*
> *Holder of heaven and earth,*
> *Open our hearts that we may hear Thy voice*
> *Which constantly comes from within.*
> *Disclose to us Thy divine light*

Which is hidden in our souls,
That we may know and understand life better.
Most merciful and compassionate God
Give us Thy great goodness,
Teach us Thy loving forgiveness,
Raise us above the differences and distinctions that divide
    people,
Send us the peace of Thy divine spirit
And unite us all in Thy perfect being.[25]

4   Explore silent prayer — prayer without words. What does this mean for you? How do you experience praying without words? Can you experience how your naturally occurring presence can itself be a prayer? You might feel this as an openness of heart, a kind look in your eyes, an unspoken presence of blessing or gratitude, often not even noticed by others.

While these are solo exercises, you may wish to speak about your experience with them with someone you are close to.

· 8 ·

THE ART OF
AWAKENING

This thing we tell of can never be found by seeking, yet only seekers find it.

—ABU YAZID AL-BISTAMI, NINTH-CENTURY SUFI

Looking for it, the vision cannot be seen: cease your search. It cannot be discovered through meditation, so abandon your trance states and mental images. It cannot be accomplished by anything you do, so give up the attempt to treat the world as magical illusion. It cannot be found by seeking, so abandon all hope of results.[26]

—SHABKAR LAMA, NINETEENTH-CENTURY TIBETAN TEACHER

At this point in our work together we turn to explore more directly the paradoxical nature of awakening; in other words, of finding what we are seeking. We will encounter ever more contradictory statements such as the lines above from Bistami and Shabkar. Ultimately, however, we will be forced to abandon words altogether and simply open ourselves to this intimate space that is forever present before thoughts appear or words take shape, and after they vanish. In either case, our explorations are by necessity immediate, experiential, and direct. We cannot just think about these matters and presume to know what they mean. Direct experience without the intermediation of thought is the heart of our practice.

Contradiction will be our companion in this chapter. Statements will be made, reminders will be given, and we will learn ever more precisely to point out to ourselves the heart of the matter; at the same time, however, the *transactional* nature of those statements, reminders, and pointers (e.g., "this should be noticed," "that should be opened to," etc.,) will always need to be released. We are learning to practice the art of awakening, and essential to that art is the realization that there is no awakening, no art, and nothing to practice.

THE IDEA THAT SOMETHING IS MISSING

From the consensus view of reality, life in general, and our individual lives in particular, are in constant need of repair. Things are not as we wish them to be. We are cold and we need to put on a sweater. We are lonely and we need loving contact. Nations are in conflict and need to live in peace. Something almost always seems to be missing, except for short moments when desire is fulfilled, and these moments evaporate rapidly. Our bottom-line experience is that everything is in a continual state of incompletion. This is the reality from the perspective of dualistic perception, and these human bodies of ours are exquisitely designed to perceive dualistically.

The paradox we face in opening to nondual awareness is that while our ordinary dualistic view is useful for survival purposes, it produces a considerable amount of confusion and turbulence in our lives when it is mistaken for fundamental truth. This becomes clear as we recognize the provisional nature of identifying ourselves as separate, individual selves. As we have seen, the idea that I am a separate, individual self is shored up by the commonly sensed feeling that something is missing.

This is evident not only in the everyday experiences of our lives, but also in the dynamics of the spiritual path and of spiritual practice. I am a seeker and I aspire to the goal of spiritual realization. I am missing something. My experience of life could be better. I want to feel close to God. I want to find the meaning behind this existence. I want to be at peace with myself and be a loving presence in the world. These feelings may draw me to a formal religion or to a spiritual path where I hope to find what is missing — a belief system, an inspiring teacher, a community, or a practice that will assuage my sense of lack.

Implicit in this construction is the expectation that I could someday possess these qualities even though I feel their absence now. If we look closely we can see how this gaining idea once again refers back to and reinforces the sense of the separate I. For example, by making myself sit still in meditation, trying to tame the thoughts and emotions that arise in my awareness, I hope to finally gain what I lack, i.e., a calm mind. I will be *more* than I was. Here we see how taking on spiritual practices can be counterproductive. Instead of releasing the sense of self, they reinforce it. Instead of resolving the subject-object duality, they employ it. Instead of opening my awareness to the ineffable mystery of existence, they give me ways to define it.

And yet it would be an error to dismiss the entire religious and spiritual curriculum of humanity because many of its expressions become caught in the same attachments they seek to free us from. Despite the pitfalls described above, spiritual practice *can* serve a positive function. We see evidence for this in the experiences of illuminated souls throughout history. *But what does it take for spiritual practice to be effective?*

THE ART OF AWAKENING

If we approach the process of spiritual awakening as an art rather than as a discipline or a series of manipulative practices, we may be able to avoid the gaining ideas that cloud it. All art requires discipline, yet discipline alone does not produce art. Great art arrives through the artist's openness to the unknown and the unexpected, in addition to his or her history of practice and developed skills. In the same way there is a *ripening process* whereby spiritual teachings and practices can serve to bring us to a readiness from which we may more easily open *beyond* preparation, and path, and ripening.

We can appreciate how all the teachings we have been exposed to, plus all the practices we may have experienced in our lives — sitting in silence, watching our breath, repeating mantra, praying, inquiring into the nature of the self, responding to koans, etc. have helped ripen us in two basic ways. First, they have encouraged us to consider the *possibility* that we are not a separate self, but may in fact be one with the transparent and radiant awareness that is the ground of being. This is initially an intellectual consideration — we are invited by teachings and practices to relax our assumptions about what is real. We allow for the possibility that reality may not be as we had imagined. We allow for the possibility that the familiar awareness we experience as the essence of our everyday perception is somehow continuous with the boundless awareness that is the essence of everything.

These kinds of insights have increased our capacity to be comfortable with not knowing answers and not needing to know. They have helped us give up trying to define the world and ourselves. They have helped make room for the ineffable.

The second way in which spiritual teachings and practices serve to ripen us is by helping to *clarify* the internal stresses of our mental and emotional life. By "clarify" I mean their capacity to help us reduce the speed and volume of thoughts, become aware of habitual patterns of thinking, release attachments and identifications, and to open our hearts. From this perspective we can see how a path of practices can create conditions in our lives from which we are more likely to recognize our identity with the clear light of open awareness.

Through both of these functions — revealing the *possibility* of our true nature and *clarifying* our mental and emotional environment so that we may be better able to realize that nature — spiritual practices can serve us on our path. As long as they emphasize these two functions, they will not mislead us. Teachings and practices must be utterly humble in this regard, recognizing their limits, not implying that they are indispensable keys required to unlock the mystical door, but are more like the stillness of the night air that allows the pond's surface to reflect the moon. At their best, spiritual practices subtract from our self-concept, reducing the turbulence of the pond's surface, not adding to it.

This image suggests that teachings and practices are useful to the extent they prepare us to notice what is already true. When we finally *recognize* this that is already true, we realize it's been here all along, and no preparation was necessary to recognize it. As we continue in this work it is crucial we not lose sight of this paradox, that we hold lightly all of our language about "awakening" and an "art of awakening," recognizing how easy it is to believe these words represent something that is special in itself, or that we are special to pursue it. As we know, any idea of specialness can obscure our opening into the identityless presence of being.

The reason I am introducing the notion of an *art of awakening* here is in recognition of the fact that, for the great majority of us, the process of opening into the identityless presence of being is not a one-time event. It is ongoing. One day we may experience a glimpse of the invisible presence of open awareness, finding that we are resting easily in its clear and spontaneous light. The next day we may experience ourselves as heavy, wooden, and full of conflicting thoughts. This simply happens, the result of decades of habituating tendencies. So we can relax, learning to play creatively with ways to release our attachments to thoughts, beliefs, and preferences. Rather than expecting final attainment, we become artists of our own awakening.

PRACTICING THE ART

Since the intention of this chapter is to offer some approaches that may contribute to an art of awakening, I have included here in the text suggestions for exercises and forms of inquiry rather than listing them in a separate "Exercises" section at the end of the chapter.

What does it mean to be the artist of your own awakening? What are the moves of your dance?

Of course, these "moves" might consist of any of the practices suggested in this book: the practice of subtle opening, noticing and deconstructing fixations, working with inquiry, prayer, and other ways. But most importantly, each move you explore will require being completely sincere in your presence to this work, and engaging it on an original, creative, on-going basis. You must make it your own. The teachings and pointers of the Open Path, and in the great nondual traditions represented in the books listed in the bibliography, can be used by you as a host of reminders — in whatever ways work for you — to suggest the directionless direction that opens you to your natural condition, the transparency of pure awareness that you are.

So far in this book we have immersed ourselves in both functions of spiritual teachings and practice described above: *opening to the possibility* of the extreme intimacy of the truth; and *clarifying* the mind stream through observing and releasing mental and emotional fixations, calming the traffic of thought, and learning to recognize the insubstantiality of thoughts in their arising and passing. Now you must begin to explore these functions in your own creative ways. They work not because someone told them to you, but because they begin to arise from your own unrelenting inquiry.

I want to repeat: this is an ongoing process. No matter how clear our recognition of the selfless, open nature we share with all being, identifications and attachments inevitably arise in our mind stream. The opportunity to see through them gives us the chance to practice our art every day. It takes continuous and subtle discernment. It takes our being open to reminders as they arise from the teachings we hear or have heard in the past. Even more, it takes the power of our own inquiry and steadiness, again and again opening to the re-membrance of what we are.

Of course, this remembering, this reminding, is still in the realm of "practice." It is the preamble to awakening, not awakening itself. But saying that is also misleading. To speak of practices as a preamble to an event called awakening is only provisionally helpful. Ultimately practices cannot lead us to awakening. In fact, there is no awakening! The nature of everything is awake already. But even that is not quite true. To say anything at all about "this thing we tell of" complicates our minds.

The preceding paragraph is one example of what I mean by prac-ticing the art of awakening. It is an art that is practiced by pointing to nothing, by releasing all conclusions, and by inviting our aware-ness to rest in what it is, this contentless clearing.

In the remainder of this chapter we will consider three possible elements of the art of awakening.

CONVERSATIONS THAT RELEASE

Imagine you are sitting silently, doing nothing. After a while you re-alize you are looking for something. You are looking for *This*, for pure unconditioned awareness, the sense of clear spaciousness and natural ease you felt at sometime in the past. You notice the experience of "looking for It" arising in your awareness, and feel the pull it has on you. You notice also the sense of being the one who looks, of peering through thoughts and sensations looking for open awareness. Now what arises naturally in your mind stream may be a series of reminders like the following, interspersed with long pauses and silence:

> *I wonder what it really is that is doing this looking? What is it that receives the data from looking? I think I should look for that!*
> Silence.
> *What is this looking process anyway? It needs a subject, me, who looks, and a process of looking, and an object looked at. This "looking" feeling is keeping my awareness split into a subject-object set-up. Who's looking?*
> Silence.
> *I wonder if I don't look, what would happen? How would I ever find it if I don't look?*
> Silence.
> *I don't know. Oh well.*
> Silence.
> *I can't remember what I'm looking for anyway. It's supposed to be open awareness, but what's that?*
> Silence.
> *I remember it's no different from the awareness I experience right now. What is this awareness now?*
> Silence.
> *Oh.*

You are probably familiar with this kind of internal conversation. If it runs away with itself, it can easily become a kind of nervous habit of thoughts talking to themselves. However, it can also be a useful process of releasing patterns of thinking and feeling that are unnecessary elaborations on your direct experience. The key to keeping such releasing conversations useful is to allow them to always proceed toward "nothing," toward spaciousness, toward identityless-ness, toward unconditioned awareness. (However, by using the word "toward" a directionality is implied when there actually isn't one. It is more properly speaking a "directionless direction.") Played with discernment and responsiveness, this kind of "conversation" is an aspect of the art I am talking about.

While the internal conversation above is carried out with words and thoughts, the art of it can be even more effective when it proceeds as a kind of inner kinesthetic nonverbal movement "from openness to openness" as the field appears. Or you may need only to use a particular key word or phrase that holds power for you to effect release. Phrases such as "listen to listening," "open into openness," "wait without waiting," and "keep to the first moment," or prayer phrases like "ya latif" can initiate a kinesthetic movement that allows your experience and presence to open from imagining it is contained in a specific reference point to recognizing the spaciousness of its true nature.

It also may be helpful to realize that these kinds of releasing conversations are nothing other than a spontaneous process of listening to inner guidance. We actually don't "do" anything in these inner conversations or short reminders. We are not figuring anything out. A natural intelligence is ever-present as we learn to relax from thinking we know something. We just listen, or rather, listening just happens, and in this completely natural way the mind's tendency to hold onto beliefs and conclusions is noticed and the mind relaxes. The essence of the art of awakening, as the essence of any art, is spontaneity. Guidance naturally comes. Noticing happens. Awakening opens in spontaneous surprise.

DEVELOPING A NON-DOING
CONTEMPLATIVE PRACTICE

We have already been exploring the experience of "non-doing" in the practice of subtle opening and in the river flow meditation. I would like to suggest, when you feel you are ready, that you take on *non-doing contemplation* as a core aspect of the art of awakening you practice. You may wish to alternate it with other practices that you are familiar with and enjoy doing, or shift back and forth from the kind of releasing conversations described above, and the forms of self-inquiry described in chapter five, to non-doing contemplation as the weather of your mind and emotions changes, and as you feel the need for reminding. This is your art.

Here are a few abridged paragraphs from the description of non-doing in chapter two:

> How do we do non-doing? By relaxing naturally, though remaining quiet and alert, and in an alert posture, as we have been for the previous parts of the practice. This is the Sufi teacher Inayat Khan's description of meditation: *mystical relaxation.* No effort. Even no effort at having no effort. We are simply still and present. What arises, arises. What passes, passes.
>
> If we notice that we have become involved in what arises — thoughts or emotions — we don't bother about it, we simply notice it and allow it to pass without our further involvement. Non-doing is pure witness. We produce no interference with what occurs.
>
> *Since effort — which creates causes and effects, whether positive or negative — is unnecessary, immerse yourself in genuine being, resting naturally with nothing needing to be done. The expanse of spontaneous presence entails no deliberate effort, no acceptance*

or rejection. From now on make no effort, since phenomena already are what they are.

—LONGCHENPA

Many people have difficulty with *non-doing*. Even when we reduce our outward "doing" to an absolute minimum (sitting upright and still), inwardly the mind compensates by "doing" at a fierce rate. Since most of us are largely identified with our mind stream, this tends to make the practice of non-doing frustrating. *I can't stop doing my mind stream!*

Here we might benefit from some advice of the great Hindu teacher Sri Nisargadatta Maharaj as he responds to a questioner who complains, "My thoughts won't let me rest."

> Pay no attention. Don't fight them. Just do nothing about them, let them be, whatever they are. Your very fighting them gives them life. Just disregard. Look through....You need not stop thinking. Just cease being interested. It is disinterestedness that liberates. Don't hold on, that is all. The world is made of rings. The hooks are all yours. Make straight your hooks and nothing can hold you. Give up your addictions. There is nothing else to give up. Stop your routine of acquisitiveness, your habit of looking for results, and the freedom of the universe is yours. Be effortless.[8]

Non-doing is actually a kind of non-practice. Fundamentally you are not doing anything, just abiding in your natural quiet attention. You are clear-headed. You have no agenda. Nothing has to change or get better. You're no longer looking for anything. There is no one looking. There is just this welcoming, this openness. It is alert and accepting of what comes. Thoughts arise. Feelings and sensations arise. You let them be. You are simply not interested in pursuing them. They vanish. All thoughts, emotions, and sensations dissolve naturally into open awareness.

You recognize you are not a "you," but simply awareness aware of what is happening. You don't have to do anything to have this be so — it is the very nature of what you are. It is completely nonpersonal. There is multi-dimensional listening and seeing, but no center. You are no longer identified with being your mind, or for that matter, your body. No identification is necessary. There is only *This that is*.

In my experience it is helpful to maintain a fairly steady diet of non-doing contemplative practice — perhaps twenty minutes a day, although allowing a number of periods of non-doing throughout your day is even better. As non-doing becomes more familiar to you, you will find yourself opening into its openness more often, while waiting in line, or driving, or sitting talking with friends. Non-doing does not mean you cannot perform daily functions, although you may want to extend your non-doing practice from its secluded, meditative setting to social settings gently. It simply means living selflessly, with direct perception, open to whatever comes while holding on to nothing. Actions take care of themselves, arising out of the natural intelligence of each situation. Words are spoken when they are called for. You are this self-arising presence and its flow of movement and responsiveness, without having to devise anything.

RELEASE AT INCEPTION

A helpful adjunct to the non-doing contemplative practice is the three aspects, or recognitions, involved in the Tibetan Dzogchen "pointing out instruction" called *release at inception*. This is a subtle practice, so subtle that it is not actually a practice but could be described more accurately as a series of appreciations of what is naturally occurring. You may find that these recognitions take frequent experimentation for them to feel natural. Yet they essentially involve no effort — simply noticing *what is* without adding any interpretation.

The three recognitions are described below. The descriptions are my own interpretation and are not necessarily how the Tibetans conceive them. You may wish to contemplate these aspects and take them into the intimacy of your own practice. As with the non-doing contemplative practice, these reminders can be recalled at any time, not only when you are sitting in meditation.

It could be said that the purpose of the recognitions of *release at inception* is the dissolving of the subject-object relationship. With these recognitions our fascination with and attachment to thoughts, emotions, and sensory impressions dissolves. Our sense of their substantiality dissolves. We notice how all appearances, all phenomena — including our bodies and all feelings of selfhood — are inseparable from the boundless context of empty awareness in which they appear. As we become more familiar with this recognition, we sense a profound detachment from the things of life that had previously entranced us. This is not a conceptual state, but an experience in the moment. At the same time, we sense a clarity and immediacy of encounter with "the things of life," although now we are no longer attached to them. There is intimacy rather than clinging.

These three recognitions or appreciations are not intended as a sequential practice. They reveal each other without any effort on your part, and they could just as easily be seen as one recognition with different facets, like a single jewel.

1. THE COINCIDENCE OF AWARENESS AND OBJECTS

Allow your mind and body to settle in a relaxed, natural, alert state. The instructions for the non-doing contemplative practice are relevant here. Simply leave your awareness as it is, without contriving anything in your mind, neither blocking nor pursuing any thought, emotion, or sensation. Be at ease in the natural openness you are.

Now, whatever arises in your awareness — whether it is an appearance of external objects such as forms, sounds, smells, etc., or an appearance of internal mental or emotional activity — at the very moment of its appearance, notice the point of union between your awareness and what is appearing. This is sometimes called "the first moment." Notice that whatever is arising in the first moment is coincident with your awareness. This is the entire instruction. There is actually nothing you are doing here, simply noticing the coincidence of perceived objects with your awareness. You don't have to objectify your awareness, thinking of it as some "thing." Just notice that awareness coincides with whatever appears.

By recognizing thoughts, emotions, and sensations just as they are, as they appear — at their point of union with awareness — their "charge," whether conceptual or emotional, is released. Whatever potency and fascination they hold is released.

One of the challenges of this noticing is to keep flowing with it. You will experience that one thing arises after another: a sensation, a thought, an emotion, another thought, another sensory impression. Just relax in the first moment of this flow of appearances, without doing anything extra. If you notice you have started to endorse and amplify a certain thought that arises, or an emotional energy that arises, just see that without comment or reaction. You always have a field in which to engage with this practice.

You will experience that if this simple recognition of appearances, just as they are, does not occur, then an ordinary oblivious state of mind results. You may daydream, or become entranced in other ways with what appears. You may comment on it and have opinions about it. This commentary then creates a space in which self-concept thrives — the "ordinary oblivious state of mind."

As you experiment with this practice you may feel it produces a sense of detachment from the world and all the things that "matter" to you. This may be uncomfortable at first — some people retreat from this feeling of detachment because it can initially feel like a loss of the juice of life. I can only encourage you to open yourself to it. The clarity and intimacy it makes possible will soon become evident to you.

You may also experience that this sense of detachment begins to form a feeling of being a witness. As I have mentioned in another context, witness-consciousness can be a helpful interim step in freeing yourself from identification with what's happening, but if reinforced it can easily become another hideout for the ego. In the context of this practice of seeing the coincidence of awareness and objects, it is simplest to see the formation of the witness as just another appearance. It will dissolve of its own accord.

2. No Trace

The second facet of *release at inception* occurs as you recognize that all experience vanishes without a trace. Whatever occurs is seen as it is (the coincidence of awareness and objects), and then vanishes "like a bird's flight-path in the sky." Appearances reach their fullness in your direct perception, and then you notice they immediately dissolve of their own accord, disappearing in the "indeterminate space of pristine awareness." This happens by itself — you don't do anything to make it happen. It is the natural spontaneity of the universal moment. There is no time in which this happens.

You might suspect that this continual disappearing of what appears would make everything stop, or that there would be no memory and thus nothing would be learned. But it is just because everything is released at inception that the universe continues becoming. And we see spontaneous "learning" everywhere, as the vine grows toward the light without commentary, and the bird swoops through the trees and avoids the branches without commentary. Just so can we live, free of obsessive thoughts about past and future. A natural intelligence guides everything spontaneously, without deliberation, just as a baby grows in the womb without deliberation.

In this recognition you may also experience yourself vanishing along with everything else. The positioning that occurs when you endorse a belief or opinion or emotion vanishes just as effortlessly as the things that appear in your vision vanish when you turn your head. When you first experience this, it can be stunning, or even a little scary. Where am I? What can I hold on to?

Here the only advice is to relax and let be. The clear spaciousness we are, dawns. There is no trace of neediness or fear of loss. Nothing needs to be done.

3. UNITY

The third facet of *release at inception* is the spontaneous appreciation that every appearance of any object, sensation, thought or emotion, every movement in awareness, arises, abides, and is released in the wide-open unitary spaciousness of being, like "another wave in the ocean." The realization here is of the unity of everything. Relative and absolute, conditioned and unconditioned, material and immaterial, faults and virtues are the same in spaciousness. It is as if the surface of the shoreless ocean of light shimmers with infinite little waves — these forms, sounds, textures, colors, thoughts, and emotions that we experience — while nothing is separate from the light. Every wave and ripple arises and disappears, and is never anything other than this shoreless ocean of infinite generosity.

As we recognize this facet, we recognize our unity with the ocean. This is our own true face. We realize that everything is all right and has been all right forever. We, and everyone and everything and every occurrence that has ever occurred — even the worst things we can imagine — have never left the compassionate emptiness of the clear light.

CONCLUSION

The art of awakening does not consist of any specific methods or practices, neither the particular brush strokes suggested in this chapter, nor any other menu of suggestions. It is a living art that is performed in the same way a tree's branches move in the wind. My hope is that you will become your own creative artist of awakening — curious, experimental, and honest moment by moment, remembering that while you give yourself totally to your art in these and many other ways, no effort is needed.

· 9 ·

A JOYOUS
COSMOLOGY

INTRODUCTION

As we explored in the previous chapter, "The Art of Awakening," it can be helpful to have some intimate points of guidance or remembrance to serve our art. As we proceed on the Open Path, we find examples of these reminders — sometimes from teachings or scripture or poetry, sometimes from experiences in the natural world, sometimes from a more invisible source within the moment. In this chapter, "A Joyous Cosmology," I would like to share with you four themes that can serve us in this way.

I have taken the basis of these themes from a treatise known as *The Precious Treasury of the Way of Abiding*, written by the fourteenth-century Tibetan master Longchenpa, and from one of his sources, the early Dzogchen scripture known as *The Supreme Source.*[27] What follows, however, is not intended to be a report on Longchenpa's teachings on this subject. It is my own improvisation on these ancient themes, and reflects my interest in exploring how these exquisite mystical realizations may land in our own experience of life.

This chapter covers a lot of ground, and since you may find it easier to read section by section, I include here a table of contents of its headings and sub-headings:

Theme I: Realizing the Absence of Story
  The Nature of Thoughts and Feelings
  The Nature of Awareness
  The Nature of the Real World
  The Face of Absence

Theme II: Experiencing the Intimacy of Openness
  What is Openness?
  Opening into Openness
  The Intimacy of Openness

Theme III: Surrendering All at Once

Theme IV: The Joy of Unbounded Wholeness
  Awareness as the Wholeness of the One
  Awareness as Spaciousness Itself
  The Oneness of Being Does Not Follow from a Cause
  The Oneness of Being Reveals Itself as Pure Enjoyment and Endless Variation

This is the longest chapter in this book, and admittedly not the easiest to read. Nevertheless, much of this material refers to aspects of our work that we have focused on earlier, which we now can explore at a deeper level. As you will see, I have used a number of styles — some conversational, some poetic, some quite dense, and I have interspersed poetry where I could. I suggest you read the chapter slowly and in several sittings rather than trying to digest it all in one meal. If you can't follow all of this, don't worry. Just let the words be like a river you swim in, and return to them once in a while when you feel like taking a dip.

As you know, the Open Path is not a religion and does not involve learning or agreeing with a particular doctrine or metaphysical system. As much as possible, in our explorations of the Open Path we stay focused on the evidence of our immediate experience. I realize that in calling this chapter "A Joyous Cosmology," it may appear that I'm inviting us into some kind of metaphysical speculation, but that's not my intention. The purpose of this chapter is to offer a number of ways to contemplate — mostly through direct inquiry and poetry — the nature of reality. If it tends to induce a lot of thinking for you, put it down. If it suggests openings for you into direct experience beyond these words, then it has served its purpose.

THEME I: REALIZING THE
ABSENCE OF STORY

This first contemplation considers the nature of *absence*, looking at what this word signifies in two distinct ways. The first is to regard absence as one side of a dualistic equation: the presence of something and the absence of something, in this case the absence of story (i.e., mental and emotional constructions). Within the context of conditioned reality, of seeking to free ourselves from identification with stories, this dualistic meaning is accurate and has some benefit. But in an unconditioned nondual context, the word *absence* signifies a quality that is much less tangible; in fact, it is not tangible at all. Instead it carries the implication of "emptiness" — as in an empty sky or as in the sense of pure capacity like an empty bowl. The bowl is a bowl because of the emptiness it allows. In an analogous way we can appreciate that the wholeness of reality can *be* because of the emptiness that is intrinsic to it.

THE NATURE OF THOUGHTS AND FEELINGS

When we sit quietly, doing nothing, we notice that thoughts or feelings appear and then disappear in our awareness. When we look carefully we also notice the curious fact that this intermittent stream of thoughts or feelings seems to appear out of nowhere — that is, the thoughts or feelings are at one moment completely absent or unfindable, and then they appear! You can check this at any time with any thought or feeling that arises — simply try to see if the thought or feeling has any findable origin before it occurs to you.

Taking this a step further, we can notice that the thoughts or feelings that arise in our awareness also seem to constantly transform or disappear — they don't exist immutably. What happens to them? Where do they go when they are no longer present in our awareness, or when their appearance changes? Again, it seems their original appearance or quality disappears into "nowhere."

Now if we look at a thought or feeling itself when it seems to be present in our awareness, can we actually find it? For example, consider the thought of "finding." We know what the word means but can we find that meaning when we look for it? I'm not referring to its definition; I am referring to the seeming existence of the thought "finding." Try to find it. Notice that it actually vanishes instantaneously when you try to "find" it. You can't find finding! You can't even find not finding! This is true of any thought or feeling that arises — they don't actually exist as objects you can find or make hold still or inspect. They vanish, or they transform into something else.

Try this with the thought, or the feeling, of "me," of your primary sense of subjectivity. Look to see if you can find where it comes from just before you become aware of it. Now look to see if you can find where it goes when you no longer think about it or feel it. And now look to see what it is, precisely when you *are* thinking about it or feeling it. It would be best if you actually take a few moments now to do this exercise — and the others that are suggested along the way — rather than assuming you know what they reveal. This will help give all these words a grounding in your direct experience.

You may notice that in all cases — in its origin, its destination, and in its seeming existence as something in itself — the actual thought or feeling of "me" is unfindable. I realize this may sound unreasonable, even ridiculous. But I encourage you to be the scientist of your own experience and see for yourself — don't take my word for it. When you look for the reality or substantiality or straightforward existence of the feeling or thought of "me," what happens? What do you find?

It is helpful to go slow here. Repeat the line of inquiry just described at your own pace, and as many times as you need to. Indeed, this exploration can be repeated usefully over several days, weeks, months, or years.

You might think it makes no sense to say you can't find the thought or feeling of "me," or where it comes from, or where it goes. It comes, you might say, from the whole interlocking system of linguistic conditioning and development of self-concepts we have painstakingly learned from an early age. Yes, we could use this story as an explanation of "me," but it still doesn't change the fact that when we look for a "me," we cannot find it. Isn't this explanation simply another thought? Where was this thought before it appeared? Where is it after it disappears? Where (and what) is it when it is present? If you try to find this story-thought you come up empty-handed. It, in itself, and in its origin and destination, is absent. It has no definitive nature or constancy. When you try to touch it or report accurately about it, you discover its nature is both ephemeral (not lasting) and ineffable (not able to be expressed in words), just like every other thought or feeling you might have.

It may be that you have followed this line of inquiry this far, but then say, "So what?" It may seem to you that this is nothing more than a philosophical or linguistic trick that has no relevance to how we live our lives, or to what is actually true. Here, once again, you need to go very slowly. If the actual nature of thoughts and feelings is both ephemeral and ineffable, then we have to admit they have no reality in themselves — that is, they can be nothing more than a vivid display of absence. They arise from absence, they disappear into absence, and inasmuch as they "exist," they exist as an ephemeral and momentary display, not as things in themselves that remain stable or constant in any describable way.

The implication of this revelation is that the entire vast interwoven fabric of stories by which we describe reality and ourselves — all the judgments, discriminations, elaborations, the placing of events in the past or the future, all determinations of causality, all descriptions of good and bad, right and wrong, blame and credit — these are actually ephemeral "displays" arising from a matrix of absence or emptiness. They have no substance or fixed attributes in themselves. They are stories, and as stories their nature is absence. That is, they are empty of, devoid of, an identity that has any fixed characteristics.

Stop now and allow this realization time to sink in. It implies that our thoughts and feelings are only provisionally accurate. They do not really exist, just as their "meaning" or story does not really exist. They are momentary signs, like dreams, that do not exist independently in themselves. Realizing this doesn't mean we no longer give credence to our thoughts and emotions or the stories they signify. We can recognize them for the relative meaning they point to, and act on that meaning if appropriate, but now we see through them. This seeing-through releases us from any attachment we may have to their ultimate significance. Because we see that their essence is absence — emptiness rather than substance — we are freed from their dominance.

THE NATURE OF AWARENESS

Now let us take another approach to this same revelation of the absence of stories. This is an approach you are familiar with by now in the work of the Open Path. As you sit quietly, doing nothing, see if you can find the nature of your awareness. You know it is the ground of your being, since without it — whatever it is — there would be no chance to notice or explore anything, including your "being." But what is this awareness? Does it have any attribute? Color? Texture? Center or periphery? Front or back? Is it visible in any way? Does it have any basic feeling tone? Can you find if it begins somewhere or sometime, or ends somewhere or sometime? Can you discover if it is inside you and not outside you? Where is it? Does awareness have a story? Or is it also the absence of story?

We are already familiar with this kind of questions, but it is helpful to go through this inquiry often, letting it become part of your daily exploration over a period of time. Even though I will continue our inquiry here and suggest possible revelations arising from it, it is important that you not take my word for it, but proceed through the inquiry yourself until you have come to the certainty of your own experience.

Not surprisingly, this inquiry brings us to the direct realization that the nature of awareness itself cannot be expressed. Its nature is ineffable, unutterable. While we can be absolutely convinced of awareness's presence or reality, we can't say what that reality or presence is. It is ungraspable, in the same way we discovered that the thoughts and feelings that appear in our awareness are ungraspable.

The implications of seeing awareness itself as absent of story are profound, as we have come to recognize throughout this work. Every aspect of reality as we know it is united with the emptiness or "absence" that is the essence of awareness.

THE NATURE OF THE REAL WORLD

This unity is most evident when we consider the reliability or reality of the information received through our senses. A radical deconstruction of the stories we have built upon the data provided by our senses can undermine the seeming solidity of our world. However, this is a much more challenging deconstruction than an inquiry into the substantiality of thoughts, feelings, and awareness. Our certainty in the reality of the objects of the world "out there" is rooted in our evolution as biological organisms. If we challenge the ultimate reality of the subject-object dichotomy, the suspicion is we may no longer be careful. We might think that if reality is perceived as one whole, we would no longer feel the need to protect ourselves from a part of it.

But beyond this, our certainty in the reality of physical phenomena seems just common sense. You can imagine yourself slamming your fist on a table and saying, "This is real!" You can imagine seeing a truck speeding directly toward you and saying, "This is real!" You can imagine holding a small child in your arms and saying, "This is real!"

With this basic predisposition we have toward the fundamental reality and existence of supposedly external objects, any attempt at deconstructing this predisposition faces an enormous challenge. My sense is that to be able to see through the apparent substantiality of objects we need to begin with the kinds of deconstruction inquiry mentioned above, focusing first of all on the absence of the substantial identity of thoughts and feelings, and on the direct recognition of the nonsubstantiality of awareness. When we become convinced of the "emptiness" of thoughts, feelings, and of awareness itself, through our own experience, then the idea of a "real world" out there becomes less solid.

For now I will mention this possibility only briefly, and return to it in the subsequent themes. Here it may be enough to suggest that, since every experience of every phenomenon of "the real world" appears — and can only appear — in the context of awareness, then in some way the reality of the world, its apparent existence, is indivisible from the ineffable, unutterable, insubstantial nature of awareness. If awareness is fundamentally coincident with absence — that is, it cannot be defined by any story — then all the stories that appear in it, e.g., the reality of trucks and babies and tables, cannot help but participate in the presence of absence.

Take a moment to see if you can find a boundary between your awareness and the phenomena that appear in it. If you are unable to do so, what does this imply for our basic assumption about reality as being defined by a subject-object structure and distinction? Is there really a world "out there?" Is there a line between inside and outside? Or could it be that supposedly physical reality is not separate from the openness (emptiness, absence, ineffability) of pure awareness? We may recall here the root phrase of the Buddha in the *Prajnaparamita Sutra (the Heart Sutra)*, "Form is emptiness; emptiness is form. Form is not other than emptiness; emptiness is not other than form."

But more important for our purposes here is not an intellectual appreciation of the possibility that all form is fundamentally empty (this is another way of saying it is absent of story), but rather, what is important for our purposes is a direct recognition of this revelation at the level of our own identity with it. That is, recognizing that my own being — this form — is emptiness. It is not other than emptiness. And emptiness — the absence of all story — is not other than my own being.

The Face of Absence

So far I have been asking you to follow a certain line of rational inquiry, and as you read along to check it with your own direct experience, looking into the nature of your thoughts, feelings, awareness, and your sensations. Because we are limited here by the narrative prose form, we may be asking this form of writing to carry more weight than it can bear. So with your help I'd like to try a more poetic variation to conclude this first section, now that we have set the stage with the preceding narrative.

Our challenge at this moment is to realize the nature of absence by letting it emerge through our direct experience, and while still reading a text. One way may be to read the following lines slowly, allowing sufficient pauses as necessary to let the sense of the lines emerge from within your experience. Ultimately, of course, we are challenging ourselves to recognize absence — the open freshness of the moment — in the spontaneous living of our lives far from any text.

> *What is the face of absence? Here in my own face that is like the sky,*
> *spacious and without center or edge, the face of absence is without an opposite.*
> *Looking for it I find nothing. But how can I tell nothing is nothing?*
> *Like the innocence of empty space before the idea of empty space has formed,*
> *in this immediacy no story can take hold and clear absence is revealed.*
>
> *But even if a story does take hold, what could it hold to?*
> *Absence.*
> *Story-maker, who are you?*
> *Absence.*
> *Absence, show your face!*
> *Here. The absence of absence.*
>
> *Each moment, phenomena rising like partridges flushed from the grass,*
> *the traces of my memory the same, the beating of wings, vanishing.*
> *Can I locate it, this awareness in which the birds rise up?*
> *And you, there, in whose awareness the birds also startle, do we share the same sky?*

To see the face of absence we must be very quick,
accepting nothing and rejecting nothing. What does this mean?
It means there is no beginning to this seeing, no end, and no
*   middle.*
No story, our language an awkward convenience.

The face of absence is my own face that I can never see.
Not seeing it, that is it. All the windows open, no house, no
*   outside.*

Spontaneously present, absence pervades everything like space does.
Every idea of myself and of you vanishes the instant it appears,
and yet we walk together like two old friends.

The face of absence is the face of the tree, the sky, the bird,
the face of absence is the ocean billowing,
the face of absence is the wind vanishing,
the face of absence is your face listening,
the face of absence is my face listening,
the face of absence is lucid simplicity,
the face of absence can never be lost or found.

Abandon deliberate acts. These are based on the story of time
*   and improvement.*
Volition obscures the face of absence. Will precludes attainment.
Relax in absence, the natural state free of intention.

Letting go of everything the face of absence
endows us with a carefree, easy mind.

No body, no soul, no religion, no dogma, no doctrine,
no before, no after, no now, free of all constraints, no stories at all,

no positions to defend, nothing to attain,
no way to think of or express this essence,
the intuition of absence reveals causeless spontaneous joy.

THEME II: EXPERIENCING
THE INTIMACY OF OPENNESS

WHAT IS OPENNESS?

The experience of openness arises with the intuition of the absence of story. As we relax our hold on concepts and the identities they provide us, we begin to open to the wonder of reality beyond anything we can imagine. Our sense of being a mortal body, of being a certain person, of having a definitive point of view on the world, of having opinions, likes, and dislikes — these familiar constructions may offer us some comfort and orientation in our lives, but they also carry with them the distress of alienation and the anxiety of trying to control our world. Now, as we allow ourselves to perceive the innate absence of these stories in reality, an ineffable quality of openness begins to dawn.

The term "openness," as we are using it here, has many dimensions of resonance. First of all, we may imagine the openness of space. Space is infinitely open. Not only can we not imagine an outer limit to its vastness, we seem equally incapable of imagining an inner limit. Similarly, we may imagine the openness of awareness. Awareness too is infinitely open. Can we find an outer limit to awareness? An inner limit? In both cases — open space and open awareness — the nature of what we are talking about is fundamentally inconceivable and unexplainable, yet these "dimensions" of our experience seem nevertheless to be characterized by an almost visceral sense of a lack of confinement. In this way the objective field (the presence of space) and the subjective field (the presence of awareness) are coincident in their openness and immediate presence.

Openness is the totality of reality, a totality without limit or closure. As there is no center to open space, there is no center to open awareness. No boundary, restriction, or limitation: this is openness. Being without limitation, reality is not even confined by space — it includes or opens into the nonspatial or that which is beyond space, just as it includes or opens into both time and timelessness.

But to become aware of what these statements mean, we cannot rely upon concepts and our normal way of knowing. Whatever the nature of openness and nonspatial and nontemporal reality is, it can be glimpsed only through our *participation* with that nature rather than our *view* of it. As Ibn al ʿArabi points out:

> In the oneness with Allah which we describe, coming close has no nearness and being far has no distance, for there is no space or time. Someone might ask, "What is being close without nearness and being far without distance?" The answer is: in one's state of closeness or farness one must realize that there is nothing but Allah. Yet you do not know yourself, because you do not know you are naught but Him. You are He without yourself. It is only when you are He without the letters and the words of knowledge that you know yourself, that you know you are the Truth.[28]

To be "without the letters and words of knowledge" is to realize the absence of story. As we have seen, this capacity is not remote from us. The very nature of our awareness in this moment is of the nature of openness and echoes the nature of the entire cosmos.

In the first theme of this chapter we contemplated how all phenomena and experience are empty of inherent story. We can see now how this emptiness or absence is another way of recognizing that all phenomena and experience are fundamentally open-ended. They are not things or experiences with separate substance. For example, you are having the experience of reading from this page right now. You might say this is an experience unto itself, relatively private and separate from the enormity of reality beyond you. But where can we draw the line between this experience of yours and the rest of the universe? Your capacity to read these words depends upon the capacity of the planet beneath you to exert gravity to hold you within its atmosphere. Gravity itself is a property of the entire universe. Similarly, the paper on which these words are printed can be present in your hands only because of the clouds that gave the rain that grew the trees over years and years that provided the pulp for the paper. Thus this moment of reading includes unknown clouds over unknown lands, and those clouds could take shape only in a world with an atmosphere formed a billion years ago, on a cooling planet spun from an exploding star in an evolving galaxy made possible by the brilliant emptiness and boundless extension of cosmic reality.

While this vision of the inseparability of all phenomena and experience is a "story," the story itself opens out beyond its parts, and we see that it is openness itself that is the narrative, an expression of infinite interdependence and immanence unconfined by space and time. And just as the entire "objective" field is present in this universal immanence, so too is the entire "subjective" field of omnipresent open awareness, with both of these dimensions simultaneous and coincident with each other. This mutual identity of the objective and subjective is what Rumi calls "God's joy:"

> *The child weaned from mother's milk*
> *now drinks wine and honey mixed,*
> *God's joy moves from unmarked box to unmarked box,*
> *from cell to cell.*
> *As rainwater,*
> *down into flowerbed.*
> *As roses, up from ground.*

Now it looks like a plate of rice or fish,
now a cliff covered with vines,
now a horse being saddled.
It hides within these,
till one day it cracks them open.[29]

OPENING INTO OPENNESS

The entire journey on the Open Path could be described with these words: *opening into openness.* Learning to recognize our original "face" of open awareness, learning to calm our mind stream, learning to notice the structure of stories and identifications that obscure our original face, learning the arts of self-inquiry and awakening, these and the other areas we have been working with all contribute to our root intention of opening into openness. And in saying it in this way, we have yet another chance to remind ourselves that all ideas of intention and methods of attaining an outcome, of learning something and changing ourselves so that we might "open," all ideas, in other words, of effort, are fundamentally misleading. This radical paradox of the Open Path has been mentioned many times, and this time will probably not be the last. However, for our purposes at the moment we don't need to revisit the implications of this paradox — we need only to relax from all trying and from all positioning of ourselves in relation to a world "out there."

Just as the word *absence* implies its opposite, so too the word *opening* implies something closed. We sense some work to do. But oddly enough, in the context of opening into nondual awareness, we come to recognize that what we thought needs opening — ourselves — is in essence already completely open. When we look directly at the nature of what we are, we see only *openness*, which, after all, is not a thing or an attribute in itself but a transparent clearing that is the heart-essence of our being and of all being. Admittedly, when we "see" openness, the transparent clearing that we are, we don't see anything. This non-seeing is attained only by relaxing —

relaxing the tendency to fixate on appearances, or to assert opinions, or to hold on to a belief in the cogency of a stream of emotion.

Relaxing in this sense is the same as opening. It means letting go into a fully receptive, free and easy state of mind. To relax is to completely cease making effort. No longer prolonging a train of association, you simply let things be as they are in the seamless openness of now. As we have seen with the contemplation on "release at inception," every thought, emotion, intention, and sensation is allowed to be just as it is without attachment or identification on our part — each event simultaneously arising and releasing exactly as it does in the undivided openness of pure being. Like the countless waves on the ocean's surface, arising and vanishing without trace, the infinite events of the universe are forever released at inception in complete relaxation.

> *So stay right here, you lucky people,*
> *let go and be happy in the natural state.*
> *Let your complicated life and everyday confusion alone*
> *and out of quietude, doing nothing, watch the nature of mind.*
> *This piece of advice is from the bottom of my heart:*
> *fully engage in contemplation and understanding is born;*
> *cherish non-attachment and delusion dissolves;*
> *and forming no agenda at all reality dawns.*
> *Whatever occurs, whatever it may be, that itself is the key,*
> *and without stopping it or nourishing it, in an even flow,*
> *freely resting, surrendering to ultimate contemplation,*
> *in naked pristine purity we reach consummation.*[30]
>
> —LONGCHENPA

THE INTIMACY OF OPENNESS

Initially, the words *absence* and *openness* may have the connotation of a quality that is both emotionally cool and conceptually abstract. As long as what these words signify is not experienced directly, they very likely will stay cool and abstract. Surely the image of stepping free of all story and interpretation into an openness without end can seem like a way of describing death. But that is not the case. As Rumi tells it:

> *This emptiness, more beautiful than existence,*
> *it obliterates existence, and yet when it comes,*
> *existence thrives and creates more existence.*[31]

Realizing the "emptiness" of absence and openness frees us from all boundaries, from all sense of personal retraction into a separate identity, or, for that matter, from all sense that the world of objects and phenomena are retracted into their own identities. This is the obliteration of existence Rumi speaks of.

Experienced directly, we recognize, in Heidegger's words, we are no more than a clearing in which the world gathers. We are an openness, completely interpenetrated with the openness of reality. This interpenetration is the most intimate experience we can ever have. It is the reality of all being, *wadhat al wujud*, "the oneness of being."

All of our work so far, these pages of words, the inquiry and deconstructions, the quiet practices — all of these are devoted to this simple recognition of intimacy. Usually we think of intimacy as requiring *two*, a relating between two entities in an intimate way. But the intimacy pointed to here is not the intimacy of two-ness, it is the intimacy of oneness. Let's let the poet Wallace Stevens conclude this section by describing this intimacy in his inimitable way:

> *Light the first light of the evening, as in a room*
> *In which we rest and, for small reason, think*
> *The world imagined is the ultimate good.*
>
> *This is, therefore, the intensest rendezvous.*
> *It is in that thought that we collect ourselves,*

Out of all the indifferences, into one thing;

Within a single thing, a single shawl
Wrapped tightly round us, since we are poor, a warmth,
A light, a power, the miraculous influence.

Here, now, we forget each other and ourselves.
We feel the obscurity of an order, a whole,
A knowledge, that which arranged the rendezvous.

Within its vital boundary, in the mind,
We say God and the imagination are one...
How high that highest candle lights the dark.

Out of this same light, out of the central mind,
We make a dwelling in the evening air,
In which being here together is enough.[32]

THEME III: SURRENDERING ALL AT ONCE

The third theme of our contemplation is the ubiquitous mystery of spontaneity. Like the nature of openness and absence, the nature of spontaneity is inconceivable and cannot be expressed by language. And like openness and absence, spontaneity has no place of its own, yet there is no place it is not. It is the totality of here and now, everywhere present, boundless, unceasing, and inexhaustible. To perceive spontaneity you need only to realize there is nothing else to perceive. In this way it remains hidden because it is the fount of all experience.

Spontaneous presence is the all-at-once-ness of reality; it is completely synonymous with open awareness, since all phenomena spontaneously appear through the avenue of awareness. Yet even though it is the totality of all phenomena, spontaneity has no spatial dimensions, no beginning or end, no inside or outside, no up or down, left or right. And though it is the very birthplace of time it is timeless, the zero-point instant that never moves, but through its infinite immediacy everything appears and is released. As an ancient text *(The Secret Tantra of the Garland of Pearls)* says, "The place of release is where it all begins." In this sense we can see that spontaneity is the essence of openness since it is the infinite potency of becoming as well as the uninterrupted and inexorable release of what appears.

Spontaneity is a word that makes a noun of the unthinkable emanation of light that is the display of all phenomena in all modes now. But even as a noun, the word *spontaneity* transforms the idea of now into a verb. Spontaneity is simultaneous presence: the simultaneity of awareness and emptiness, the simultaneity of appearance and release, and the simultaneity of light and transparence. Free of existence, spontaneity is ever absent. Free of nonexistence, spontaneity is ever present. Free of lasting, spontaneity is ever fresh. Free of not lasting, spontaneity is ever diverse. It is the generous one, the quiet one, the holy one, the free one. It is the infinite uncontrived play of spaciousness, the single endless act of uninterrupted creation. It is the only teacher, the one who reveals the nature of reality. It is the great hall of boundless clear light, the enormous sanctuary for all beings, compassion itself, the all-good. To attain spontaneity there is nothing to do. Surrendering all at once we never arrive. Without trying, leaving everything as it is, as lazy as a feather floating on the great river's back, we dwell nowhere. Surrendering to spontaneity is the key to sustaining pure unwavering awareness.

THEME IV: THE JOY OF UNBOUNDED WHOLENESS

To come to our final contemplation here on the nature of reality, we turn to the theme of *oneness* — the unified field that expresses all phenomena. Here again we cannot really speak of it, since we are whatever we are speaking of, and by speaking we make it seem to be other. Perhaps this is the first hint we can give ourselves: it is not other. Our presence in this very moment is not other than what we are contemplating. So let us consider a few of the implications of the unbounded wholeness of the one, and let us do so by inviting ourselves to look through the window of our own presence for an intimation of the oneness we are.

AWARENESS AS THE WHOLENESS OF THE ONE

As we have recognized many times, everything we experience appears in awareness, and yet when we look closely at our actual experience we cannot find a boundary between what appears in awareness and awareness itself. Thus to say "everything we experience appears *in* awareness" is not really accurate. All we can say is that awareness and the contents of awareness are inseparable — anything else is theoretical.

And as we have also recognized many times, we cannot find a boundary between awareness and whatever we might think could be outside of awareness. If we could become aware of something outside of awareness it would no longer be outside of awareness. By its very nature, awareness is unconfined. To release the story that awareness is a private matter produced by our brains opens us to the recognition of the wholeness of the one.

All phenomena share the same fundamental ground: awareness. Awareness is the single source common to everything we know. In this way, everything — every experience, phenomenon, thought, sensation, intuition, dimension, form of matter or form of energy, everything material or spiritual — is integrated in the unicity that is pure open awareness. No matter what phenomenon we name, whether judged good or bad, peaceful or vicious, right or wrong, it is undifferentiated in its essence: open awareness.

With this fundamental recognition, based on our most direct experience of reality, which is our identity with the spontaneous presence of open awareness, we begin to intuit the nature of wholeness. The image here that may help — one we have used often — is of the ocean and the infinite waves dancing on its surface. The waves, though appearing momentarily as things in themselves, are never other than the ocean. It is the same with the appearance of phenomena in the shoreless ocean of awareness. All appearances share the nature of awareness, and in that common identity the undivided wholeness of reality is revealed.

AWARENESS AS SPACIOUSNESS ITSELF

Now when we look within our own direct experience at the nature of awareness, as we have done many times, we "find" only its basic *unfindability*. The face of awareness is empty, absent, open, insubstantial, unconfined, and dimensionless — without center or edge. This means it is synonymous with spaciousness, a spaciousness that includes both external physical space and internal imaginal space, as well as the spaciousness of time and timelessness. For if we look again into our own direct experience to see if awareness is something that exists in time, with an origin and an end, we cannot find either its beginning or its dissolution. It includes all. The spaciousness of awareness embraces the entire here-and-now, but without any trace as evidence of itself.

While this talk may seem to be flirting with abstract metaphysics, it actually points to one of the most direct routes we have for recognizing the oneness of reality. Since we cannot find an edge to "our own" awareness, it is not our own. Its innate spaciousness is the spaciousness in which everything arises. Another way to say this is that the "subjective space" of awareness is identical with the "objective space" of appearances. We can have an immediate intimation of this oneness by recognizing there is no discoverable boundary between our awareness and the phenomena that appear in it. In their common spaciousness they are infinitely congruent.

The Oneness of Being Does Not Follow from a Cause

When we look at the nature of our experience right now, and throughout our life, we see that everything that happens appears to happen as a result of a cause. This is the consensus view of reality concerning how things take shape, exist, and dissolve. By this simple equation we manage our lives. However, if we look closer still, as we did in our earlier inquiry into the nature of openness, we see that we cannot reliably point to any one cause that is solely responsible for an effect — rather the entire universe throughout eternity is implicated in each event. You are able to read this sentence because the tides ebb and flow, the sun lights the heavens, and all space is spontaneous openness.

The theme of our contemplation — the wholeness of being — is revealed as we recognize the enormous implication unleashed by the simple question we asked earlier: what is it that causes you to read this sentence? Rather than a single cause, or a dozen or a hundred, we find ourselves immersed in an infinite sea of all causes and all effects. Your reading this sentence cannot be separated from anything! It is as if we stand before the spontaneous presence of all and everything and see that there is, in this ultimate view, no cause and no effect. The oneness of being does not follow from a cause, and so nothing does. Of course, it nevertheless *appears* to us that occurrences follow from causes — if we walk barefoot in the snow we get cold feet — but this is because our brains are wired to make these obviously useful interpretations, not because they are a complete representation of "reality" or how it shows up in the ways it does. Since all is one in spontaneous presence, nothing "causes" anything.

THE ONENESS OF BEING REVEALS ITSELF AS PURE ENJOYMENT AND ENDLESS VARIATION

Finally, in one last plunge into the mystery of the oneness of being and the nature of the all-embracing cosmos, let us ask this basic question: what is really happening here? And in our sincere desire to answer, let us imagine, if it were possible, that in preparation for our answer we have first been completely obliterated from existence, awareness, and being for a billion years, and then suddenly we are thrown back into existence, awareness, and being just as we are at this moment. Cleansed of all assumptions, what would we report is happening here?

I believe we would notice two facts. One, the astounding and beautiful diversity of things, the endless variation of beings, places, sounds, shapes, colors, smells, thoughts, insights, and feelings, each one distinctly unique and never repeated. And two, the single lucid indescribable sense of pure joy: the joy of being — not being something — but being being, the ineffable bliss of the oneness of being.

But let us allow Walt Whitman to answer this question for us — *what is happening here?* — and so conclude our meditation:

> *We are Nature, long have we been absent, but now we return,*
> *We become plants, trunks, foliage, roots, bark,*
> *We are bedded in the ground, we are rocks,*
> *We are oaks, we grow in the openings side by side,*
> *We browse, we are two among the wild herds, spontaneous as*
>   *any,*
> *We are two fishes swimming in the sea together,*
> *We are what locust blossoms are, we drop scent around lanes*
> *mornings and evenings,*
> *We are also the coarse smut of beasts, vegetables, minerals,*
> *We are two predatory hawks, we soar above and look down,*

We are two resplendent suns, we it is who balance ourselves
     orbic and stellar, we are as two comets,
We prowl fang'd and four-footed in the woods, we spring on prey,
We are two clouds forenoons and afternoons driving overhead,
We are seas mingling, we are two of those cheerful waves rolling
     over each other and interwetting each other,
We are what the atmosphere is, transparent, receptive, pervious,
     impervious,
We are snow, rain, cold, darkness, we are each product and
     influence of the globe,
We have circled and circled till we have arrived home again, we
     too,
We have voided all but freedom and all but our own joy.

· 10 ·

THE OCEAN
OF KINDNESS

*Is there to be found on earth a fullness of joy, or is there no such
thing? Is there some way to make life fully worth living, or is this
impossible? If there is such a way, how do you go about finding it?
What should you try to do? What should you seek to avoid? What
should be the goal in which your activity comes to rest?*[33]

—CHUANG TZU

This chapter is about discovering a reliable basis for our actions in
the world, a basis we will be describing as *unconditional kindness*.
I realize that to introduce an apparently qualitative attribute like
"kindness" into these nondual contemplations (much like the introduction of the quality of "unconditional joy" in chapter nine), I run
the risk of getting us attached to a "something." Sweet and comfort-
ing qualities with names like kindness and joy can swiftly become
objects for our mind to hold to, which we then can expect and look
for, and we can be disappointed if we don't find them.

So we have to proceed very lightly here, reminding ourselves that whatever it is we are referring to when we speak of unconditional joy and kindness, it is in essence without qualities, without structure, and without affect. I know this sounds contradictory, since joy and kindness are typically experienced affectively — we *sense* them in various ways — but it is a contradiction only on the surface. To try to describe the basic nature of reality, we can only use words that limit and objectify, and thus fall away from their intention. Our challenge is to allow words to *suggest* and then, their function fulfilled, welcome the direct realization of what they are pointing to.

We are at a point in our work together when we can release the original distinction we made between the conditioned and the unconditioned — or at least we can treat these two "realms" as transparent to each other. For now we are considering the subject of *action*, of the myriad ways we interact with this conditioned world, and we will attempt to do so from the basis of nondual awareness rather than relying upon ideas of personal responsibility — replete with assumptions of selfhood and individual will — or upon the promotion of a set of ethical precepts to guide our actions.

To restate the fundamental question of this chapter: is there a reliable basis for our actions that does not require us to abandon the lucidity and nonduality of unconditioned presence? It is not a trivial question, because on the one hand we experience ourselves immersed in conditionality with all the needs of our relationships, our work, raising children, making decisions, responding to ignorance and injustice, and generally trying to improve our world and our capacity to live the life we hope to live. On the other hand, we realize that in the most intimate, primal, and here-and-now way we are already complete. We are whole. The identity we thought we are is simply a constellation of thoughts. We are nothing other than the open, transparent awareness that is the ground of all being, this *presence* that cannot be objectified. It pervades everything, it *is* everything, and as such nothing needs to be improved, nor can it be.

Expressed in these two ways, it seems we are caught in an irreconcilable contradiction between needing to respond to our broken world and recognizing that nothing is broken. It is important for us to face into this seeming contradiction because it suggests a duality in our thinking where in fact none exists. More broadly, it brings up several interrelated and fundamental questions about action itself: Who acts? To what end? How do I act without resisting or endorsing something? How does action occur without an "I" who acts and who intends a certain outcome? Is it possible to act effortlessly? And by what light can I act so that this clear presence and ease of being is not obscured?

We will explore these questions from three vantage points, considering (1) the possibility of *nondual action*, (2) the requirement of *equanimity*, and (3) the immanence of *unconditional kindness*.

IMMANENCE

Before we begin this exploration, however, I would like to appeal once again to each of us to continually check our own present-moment experience for evidence rather than simply following along with the concepts expressed here. To say "check our own present-moment experience for evidence" simply means: look for what is immanent. Immanent means that which is inherent and in-dwelling to the nature of a thing and to the moment, and which in principle can be recognized immediately. When we look at the blue sky, blueness is immanent in this experience. It occurs before any thought we might have about blueness.

However, even though what is immanent is not hidden, we may in some cases miss this immanence because it is so obvious. For example, although the immanence of open awareness is right out front and utterly clear, it is "hidden" by its being the Only Being, or in Ibn 'Arabi's words, "That which hides It is Its Oneness." It is Rumi's "open secret."

Recognizing this "hidden immanence" is central to our contemplations as we learn to open to and sustain nondual awareness. We are recognizing that which is the essence of being at this moment, an essence without identifiable attributes — totally transparent, open, inclusive of everything, and spontaneously present. Our appreciation of just this immanent presence will be our most dependable guide as we contemplate in the following pages concepts such as "nondual action," "equanimity," and "naturally-occurring, unconditional kindness." As concepts they remain concepts — helpful to some extent but without the power of living revelation. At this time in our work together we are ready to let concepts such as these "open into openness" and be freed from their meanings so that they are no longer thoughts, but are effortlessly revealed in the immanent presence of our immanent presence.

1. NONDUAL ACTION

Let us explore first the idea of action itself, and the possibility of what may be called *nondual action*. To begin we need to acknowledge that using the word "nondual" as an adjective — in this case "nondual action" — runs the risk of making the notion of nonduality something that has an opposite, that is, nondual action as opposed to dualistic action. While we can make this distinction, let us do so provisionally, giving enough space to the idea of nondual action to allow it to be of a different order — not the opposite of anything but a possibility free of duality, a possibility immanent in the spontaneous nature of things. This allowance will help us stay in tune with what follows.

Our customary understanding of action includes the sense of there being an actor (one who initiates the action), the action itself, and the effect of the action. These three are linked together by intention. The actor intends, with his or her action, to achieve a certain outcome.

The possibility of nondual action brings this equation into question. On one hand, as we have previously explored at length, the idea of an actor who decides, intends, and initiates an action implies "a ghost in the machine," a little "self-god" who maintains the power to choose independently from the rest of the universe. On the other hand, our intention to produce a certain result embeds us in a conceptual world of expectations and attachment to those expectations.

Nondual action is action that is free of intention. Not that such *intentionless action* is aimless or random, but it simply does not situate itself in an illusion of being the product of a specific agent or in an illusion that it will result in a specific outcome. Both illusions require a certain amount of self-conscious pride or egoism: *I* am the cause of this action, and *I* define and determine its outcome.

Nondual, intentionless action is one way of describing the profound principle central to Taoism known as *wei-wu-wei*. Sometimes translated as "non-doing," *wei-wu-wei* is free of both self and intention — it is action that does not force an outcome but yields freely, like water. Also understood as nonwillful, naturally arising action, the principle of *wei-wu-wei* transcends the duality of passivity and activity, of rest and nonrest.

The ancient Ch'an (Chinese Zen) text, the *Hsin Hsin Ming* of the third patriarch, Seng-ts'an — itself deeply influenced by Taoism — echoes this understanding:

> *When rest and no rest cease to be,*
> *Then even oneness disappears.*
> *From small mind comes rest and unrest*
> *But mind awakened transcends both.*

Here what is pointed to is the possibility of action that is nonaction: movement that is simultaneously stillness. It neither arises from a cause nor culminates in an effect. We recognize the same principle expressed in the famous passage from the Hindu scripture, the *Bhagavad-gita*:

> He who in action sees inaction and action in inaction...who having abandoned attachment to the fruit of works, ever content without any kind of dependence, he does nothing though he is ever engaged in work.

To bring these insights even closer, to experience their immanence in this moment now, we might also recall the sense of *spontaneity* we explored in the previous chapter. As we relax in this moment, free from all attachment to ideas of self and the fruits of work, we may recognize ourselves as nothing other than one with the spontaneity of the whole cosmos, the spontaneity of all being, this *immanence* that cannot be pointed to because it is what is pointing. From the unspeakable spontaneity of this all-presence we may be able to explore, each in our own moment, what is suggested by the spontaneity of nonaction, the complete immanence of nondual action. Our hearts beat spontaneously without any definable cause and for no definable purpose outside of their beating. Thoughts arise in the same way, spontaneously. We look up from this page in the same way, spontaneously, for no reason. As a contemporary Zen master remarked:

> There is no reason for the "why" in anything! When we stand up, there is no reason "why." We just stand up! When we eat, we eat without any reason "why." When we put on our robe, we just put it on. Our life is a continuous just...just... just.[34]

At this point we may be able to appreciate that even when we believe we are the doer of our actions and there is a "why" for doing them, even then in the midst of supposedly dualistic action, we are not actually "doing" anything ourselves, or for the reason we believe we are. Everything always occurs "just...just...just," even our belief that it doesn't. Recognizing this, we relax from all consternation with effort and producing results. Everything that happens just does. Just this.

At the beginning of this chapter I quoted a passage from the Taoist sage Chuang-Tzu that asks: *What should be the goal in which your activity comes to rest?* This question points to the heart of our exploration here of the nature of nondual action. After commenting at length, Chuang-Tzu concludes his commentary with these words (in a rendering by the Christian monk Thomas Merton):

> *Heaven does nothing: its non-doing is its serenity.*
> *Earth does nothing: its non-doing is its rest.*
> *From the union of these two non-doings*
> *All actions proceed,*
> *All things are made.*
> *How vast, how invisible*
> *This coming-to-be!*
> *All things come from nowhere!*
> *How vast, how invisible —*
> *No way to explain it!*
> *All beings in their perfection*
> *Are born of non-doing.*
> *Hence it is said:*
> *"Heaven and earth do nothing*
> *Yet there is nothing they do not do."*[35]

To summarize, nondual action ("the goal in which your activity comes to rest") is action that is not elaborated upon by thoughts of the event being initiated by a self; it is action that does not look forward to, or claim, a specific outcome. It is motiveless. Nondual action is whole and complete in itself. Not being "done" by anyone, all action everywhere is nondual — the whole universe acts to make anything happen, or rather, *is* the action of everything happening.

The only difference between nondual action and action perceived from our usual perspective is the conceit that we are an agent and that we know what results from our agency. Released from this assumption, everything continues happening: we stretch, smile, move in the world, speak or remain silent, each act occurring freely from the tranquility of nonaction, the silence we are. It happens by itself. Like the wind moving the branches, clouds forming and vanishing, the moon reflecting in the lake, everything acts without motive or anticipation of result — an effortless dance. As T. S. Eliot tells it:

> *...at the still point, there the dance is,*
> *But neither arrest nor movement. And do not call it fixity,*
> *Where past and future are gathered. Neither movement from nor*
>   *towards,*
> *Neither ascent nor decline. Except for the point, the still point,*
> *There would be no dance, and there is only the dance.*[36]

2. EQUANIMITY

Equanimity is a word for the still point, a word that describes how this primal stillness shows up in us. Equanimity is not really something new on the Open Path that we have to learn about or practice — in fact it is identical with the essence of *openness* itself.

As we have recognized, openness is our clear, silent nature: empty, awake, and boundless. It is not contained inside our skin, but is the transparent presence of all being. As we learn to relax from our self-concepts and opinions and open into this natural openness, our lives become expressions of equanimity.

Gradually, yet without effort, we begin to notice a deepening capacity for calmness and even-temperedness. For example, rather than being propelled in conversations by the tendencies of positive and negative listening, we relax more easily into pure listening and pure speaking in which we no longer feel we have to validate or invalidate what is being said. Our identity is no longer on the line. We rest at ease in each moment, fully present and capable of offering the natural wisdom intrinsic to that presence without needing to manipulate what is happening.

We experience ourselves as centered, yet without any edge to the centeredness. This is equanimity. It is calm without any restraint of energy. It is even-tempered without being uptight. It is very relaxed, very clear, and completely open from the inside out.

The carefree ease of equanimity arises to the extent that we are able to release our attachments — our attachments to the idea of being a self-willed actor, our attachments to the fruits of our actions, our attachments to our preferences, judgments, beliefs, and opinions, and our attachments to how things unfold. Of course, while we may appreciate the concept of nonattachment and the equanimity it expresses, we may wonder how to realize this in our everyday lives. As we know, this question is at the heart of the Open Path.

Our ongoing work of recognizing repetitive mental and emotional patterns (fixations) and releasing them naturally by simply doing nothing with them is the most obvious way we respond to this question.

On an even subtler level, we have been practicing — that is, *getting used to* — the profound recognition of *emptiness*. "Emptiness" is a stark way of labeling the insubstantial nature of openness, pure awareness, and indeed, all of what we mean by reality. As we gradually get used to the radical implications of this qualityless quality that is universal emptiness, our attachments naturally fall away. The realization of emptiness and the arising of equanimity are thus united.

The fourteenth-century Tibetan philosopher Tsongkhapa points to this unity in the following three lines:

> Unborn emptiness has let go of the extremes of being and non-being. Thus it is both the center itself and the central path. Emptiness is the track on which the centered person moves.

Unborn emptiness has let go of the extremes of being and non-being. This means that we cannot say emptiness exists and we cannot say emptiness does not exist. What is represented by the word *emptiness* is not about existing or not existing. It's like this moment: we cannot say this moment exists and we cannot say it does not exist. This moment is itself empty of being something. In this way we can understand that emptiness is *unborn*: it *is* because it *is not*, and thus lets go of the extremes of being and non-being.

Thus it is both the center and the central path. This means that what is represented by the word *emptiness* is the still point, the presence-awareness of silence that is the source and destination, the alpha and omega, of every event and phenomenon. Thus emptiness is also "the central path" since everything that occurs does so through its welcoming openness.

Emptiness is the track on which the centered person moves. This line brings us back to our primary contemplation: it means that the centered person, the person firmly rooted in equanimity, moves naturally within the openness of emptiness. This is a profound point, and if you have followed me this far you will recognize it is the heart essence of what is meant by the Open Path. On this path we are guided by emptiness, or we could say, by the openness of emptiness. Free of self-concepts, beliefs, opinions, and all attachments, we are spontaneously occurring as the action of the universe.

I realize these words just barely touch our ability to realize what they are pointing to. As we know, recognizing the ineffable reality of emptiness and its implications does not depend on conceptual understanding. Stephen Batchelor emphasizes this point in his book *Buddhism Without Beliefs*:

> To know emptiness is not just to understand the concept. It is more like stumbling into a clearing in the forest, where suddenly you can move freely and see clearly. To experience emptiness is to experience the shocking absence of what normally determines the sense of who you are and the kind of reality you inhabit. It may last only a moment before the habits of a lifetime reassert themselves and close in once more. But for that moment, we witness ourselves and the world as open and vulnerable.[37]

From the basis of clear equanimity, action appropriate to the moment is spontaneously and naturally revealed. Equanimity is not a rulebook for nondual action; it is the necessary ease within which appropriate action is possible.

Although it may sound like a difficult balancing act, equanimity is utterly simple. It is simple because it does not veer from the track of emptiness — the open path that is the common spontaneous way in which all events occur. The centered person is, in Batchelor's words, "open and vulnerable," vulnerable not to threats but to the fresh openness of the moment free from clinging and judgment. And in the fresh openness of the moment we sense, without effort, the presence of unconditional kindness.

3. UNCONDITIONAL KINDNESS

I confess that I would like to sweep into the word "kindness" a whole poetry of love-words to give this common word a light we would recognize as sacred. Kindness as ultimate and unconditional love, compassion, joy, mercy, caring, gratitude, forgiveness, benevolence, blessedness. I would like this small word "kindness" to become brilliant with the radiance of all these qualities, and then name that radiance sacred, an unspeakably compassionate light inside of things utterly without cause and completely identical with what we call emptiness.

Of course, to do this would seem to give the absence that is emptiness all sorts of qualities, and I don't actually mean to do that. What I would really like to do is break through any complacency we might have that we actually know what the mystery is that we call the One, or pure open awareness, or buddha nature, or the clear light. We don't know it. It can't be known by our way of knowing things. And yet somehow in our worldly humanness we nevertheless faintly recall an endless, beginningless, infinite and ineffable light of — what shall we call it? — "unconditional kindness" behind or within everything, and that faint remembrance is what brings us here to read, and write, this sentence.

I call it "kindness" because it is a humble word that is intimate to us. Ibn al'Arabi called it *the Breath of the All-Merciful.* Garab Dorje called it *the All-Good.* Inayat Khan called it *the Perfection of Love.* Julian of Norwich called it *God's Grace.* Jack Kerouac called it *the Golden Eternity.* Countless times our ancestors have tried to represent it in words, this fundamental generosity that, each moment, gives rise to all.

However, as we have seen throughout our journey on this path, ascribing positive names like "the perfection of love" and "unconditional kindness" to the nondual nature of reality clearly runs the risk of creating consoling religious images in our mind. Words like these imply "experiences" that we may not have now but can look forward to in some future moment of revelation.

This is why most of the grammar of nondual realization avoids giving positive attributes to the "clear light of now" — *This that is.* It points only to what is immanent in this moment. It doesn't ask that we take anything on faith, it asks only that we see through all projections of the mind to the open, uncompounded presence that is awareness, this that we can't see but that we are. My own feeling is that this is the most dependable "method" for realization, because most attempts to qualify "what is realized" only become an obstacle to direct realization.

That said, I want to acknowledge that the great mystery we are opening to is not limited by any conception, not even by the conception that it is without qualities. Here we might remember the line from Ibn al'Arabi: *The journey to God is finite; the journey in God is infinite.* This is to say that emptiness, nothingness, the equanimity of complete openness is the necessary door. Passing through the door we vanish (although what vanishes has only the reality of a dream), and then what is is unspeakable. That unspeakableness is unconditional kindness, the perfection of love, the Breath of the All-Merciful, etc. It is not of the nature of things that have opposites — only by talking about it like this do we flirt with making up dualities. "It" —*This* — is the very oneness in which dualities seem to arise. Here is how Longchenpa points to it in his masterpiece, *The Precious Treasury of the Basic Space of Phenomena*:

> *Within this ultimate womb of basic space, timelessly and spontaneously present,*
> *samsara is wholly positive, nirvana is positive.*
> *Within the wholly positive expanse, samsara and nirvana have never existed.*
> *Sensory appearances are wholly positive, emptiness is positive.*
> *Within the wholly positive expanse, appearances and emptiness have never existed.*
> *Birth and death are wholly positive, happiness and suffering are positive.*
> *Within the wholly positive expanse, birth, death, happiness, and suffering have never existed.*

Self and other are wholly positive, affirmation and negation
  are positive.
Within the wholly positive expanse, self, other, affirmation,
  and negation have never existed...
Everything is wholly positive, a supreme state of spontaneous
  presence.[38]

Is there some way we can directly apprehend, immanent in this moment, that "everything is wholly positive?" Can we "see" the light of unconditional kindness, if it indeed is so fundamental to reality? I believe we can, although it too is "hidden by its oneness."

One way is to simply notice the clear empty presence of awareness, a "move" we have practiced often. Now notice that this most essential "presence of awareness" is completely *given*. It is free. Nothing needs to be done for awareness to be aware or presence to be present. Your appreciation of this given-ness may start out conceptually, but let it drop deeper into the immanence of this most basic fact: presence-awareness is given.

How is it given? What inexhaustible generosity is this?

Now notice your breathing. The air you breathe is given. It is all around you. It is composed perfectly of all the elements needed for your life to be now. And your body — notice that it too is given, and it too knows how to breathe and transform the air to fuel the metabolism of your life.

By what generosity does this occur?

The bead of semen and the waiting egg you once were long ago formed in your mother's womb your new little body, each blood vessel and nerve appearing in its place, each organ to do its job.

By what kindness in the star-filled night did this occur?

Notice light. What is it? How graciously it gives! Light made out of nothing tangible warms and colors everything, freely! How unspeakably kind it is!

This type of contemplation on the universality of "kindness" can go on and on. The point is not to label all these aspects of being with the word "kindness." The point is to simply notice that we are embraced in a miracle and we are that miracle. We might just as easily call this embrace "unconditional love" as well as "unconditional kindness." But the word "love" has been made to carry a heavy load for a long time, so we might give it a chance to rest. (The English word "kindness" comes from the Old English word meaning "natural" and "native," and carries the sense of family ["kin" and the German "Kind"] which in turn carries the sense of natural caring for family, mother love, and selfless concern for the wellbeing of others.)

The central organizing question of this chapter has been: upon what basis can we act so that our actions occur without recourse to the dualism of moral codes but simply arise naturally, in the *Tao* — the immanent current — of nondual awareness? With the preceding contemplation on unconditional kindness we can see an "answer" forming, yet our challenge, as always, is to experience this answer directly, in the nature of the moment, rather than as a conceptual conclusion.

To accomplish this, as we know, we have only to rest in the selfless emptiness of awareness. This "emptiness" is the only teacher. By it we realize our identity with the "emptiness" of all being. We realize, along with the great Zen master Dogen, that we are *nothing other than mountains and rivers and the great wide earth, the sun and the moon and the stars.* Or in the words of Jack Kerouac:

> *Discard such definite imaginations of phenomena*
> *as your own self, thou human being, thou'rt a*
> *numberless mass of sun-motes: each mote a shrine.*
> *The same as to your shyness of other selves,*
> *selfness as divided into infinite numbers of beings,*
> *or selfness as identified as one self existing*

eternally. Be obliging and noble, be generous
with your time and help and possessions, and be
kind, because the emptiness of this little place
of flesh you carry around and call your soul,
your entity, is the same emptiness in every direction
of space unmeasurably emptiness, the same, one,
and holy emptiness everywhere: why be selfy and
unfree, Man God, in your dream? Wake up, thou'rt
selfless and free. "Even and upright your mind
abides nowhere," states Hui Neng of China.
We're all in Heaven now.[39]

The entire world is our body. By learning to disidentify with our limited self-concept, we learn to identify with the whole biosphere, and beyond. It is not a learning we have to study; it is a learning that comes naturally when we cease protecting the little space of our selfness and realize our seamlessness with all being. The Norwegian philosopher, Arne Naess, in his formulation of deep ecology, calls this learning the "first ultimate norm of Self-Realization" — the nonduality of the human and nonhuman realms. From it we care, naturally, for all being. There is no need for an external code of conduct — though many have been and will be written. Recognizing that the emptiness of the universe is our emptiness, and the body of the universe is our body, the way of kindness appears by itself.

The religions of the world have codified this naturally occurring kindness in many forms. The Golden Rule appears universally and always reduces to this formula: *be kind.* Sometimes religious commandments, precepts, and laws have become twisted until they are no longer kind, but are intended to benefit one group over another, or to chastise their followers with stern rules of morality that completely lose the essence of the kindness they began with. We are all familiar with this.

This is why we have explored so carefully here "a reliable basis for our actions that does not require us to abandon the lucidity and nonduality of unconditioned presence." Most moral systems, because they rely upon polarized equations of right and wrong, can't help but obscure the lucidity of unconditioned presence. Perhaps moral codes at times in history have helped to keep the social order intact, but they have also reinforced the sense of alienation of the self and created forms of moral fundamentalism.

Nevertheless, the beauty of the light of kindness is that it can be experienced, so to speak, both unconditionally and conditionally. In the preceding pages we have explored the possibility of experiencing unconditional kindness: its immanence in the nature of things.

We can also experience kindness as a form of daily practice in thousands of ways, and by practicing kindness, in the Buddha's words, we will "soon attain highest perfect wisdom." In the exercise at the end of this chapter a few of these "kindness-practices" are suggested, and I am sure you can create many others. Either way we might explore it — through "conditional" practices or "unconditional" spontaneity — the most reliable basis for our actions is kindness.

To conclude, let us listen to another sutra from Kerouac's *Scripture of the Golden Eternity*:

> *Kindness and sympathy, understanding and*
> *encouragement, these give: they are better*
> *than just presents and gifts: no reason in the*
> *world why not. Anyhow, be nice. Remember*
> *the golden eternity is yourself. "If someone will*
> *simply practice kindness," said Gotama to*
> *Subhuti, "he will soon attain highest perfect*
> *wisdom." Then he added: "Kindness after all*
> *is only a word and it should be done on the spot*

*without thought of kindness." By practicing
kindness all over with everyone you will soon
come into the holy trance, definite distinctions
of personalities will become what they really
mysteriously are, our common and eternal blissstuff,
the pureness of everything forever, the great bright
essence of mind, even and one thing everywhere the
holy eternal milky love, the white light everywhere
everything, emptybliss, svaha, shining, ready, and
awake, the compassion in the sound of silence, the
swarming myriad trillionaire you are.*[40]

Exercise: The Ocean of Kindness

Be kind, for everyone you meet is fighting a great battle.

—PHILO OF ALEXANDRIA

Imagine — with your eyes closed — there are three people before you.[41] The first is a close friend of yours. The second is someone with whom you are very uncomfortable — an "enemy" or someone you just don't like. The third is a stranger for whom you have no feelings — perhaps the woman at the supermarket checkout.

Consider each person in turn, noticing the mood that is evoked in you by your image of each one. Your friend may make you feel secure and at ease. Your enemy may make you feel insecure and uncomfortable. The stranger may make you feel nothing at all, perhaps just polite distance.

Consider for a moment what makes you feel in these different ways toward these three people. Is it something they did in the past, or said, or how they look? Notice that you like the friend because he or she makes you feel good; that you dislike the enemy because he or she doesn't make you feel good; and that you don't care one way or another about the stranger because he or she didn't make you feel anything.

Now notice how the way you perceive these three people reinforces how you feel about them, and how you feel about them reinforces your perceptions.

Now begin to expand your perceptions. Start with your friend. Imagine him or her as a newborn baby looking up at you from her crib. Look into her eyes. Bend down and smell the fragrance of the soft hair on her head. Now try to picture her growing up from this little baby to a child: playing in the summer, sitting in school, laughing in a game, crying when she falls from her bike. Continue your imagining, picturing her as an adolescent concerned about her looks, or wondering if she is OK as a person, or dreaming about her life. See her as a young adult, falling in love, finding her way in life. Imagine her hopes, what they might have been years before you met. Imagine her as she is now, someone who values the moments of her life and her everyday feelings as much as you value yours. Now picture her growing older, becoming frail and ill, and finally picture her on her deathbed and dying.

Take your time, and do the same imagining — guided by the paragraph above — with the person you don't like and with the stranger.

Now imagine them again sitting before you, equal in birth and equal in death.

Let yourself notice how this expanded perspective has affected the way you feel about each person. You witness each one in their own right, not as how they make you feel. You see their suffering, their bravery, their disappointments and their successes. You see them joyous, the moments when they are happy with the beauty of things, and you see them grieving, when they have lost someone or something precious to them.

Now allow yourself, if you are able, to extend to each of these people in turn your sincere wish for their happiness and wellbeing. No matter what your previous feelings have been, allow yourself to wish blessings on their life, that they may realize their deepest hopes and that they will experience their lives as a benefit for their loved ones and the world.

Finally, consider how your original perceptions and feelings about these people were restrictive and selective. Recognize how you had interpreted their value according to the limits of your perceptions.

· 11 ·

THE HEART OF
THE MATTER

Wanderer, there is no path —
The path is made by walking...
Wanderer, there is no path —
only traces of foam on the sea.

—ANTONIO MACHADO

In this final chapter we circle back once again to the heart of the
matter: the recognition of the spontaneous presence of open
awareness. But first I would like to summarize our work together in
chapters six through ten (just as chapters one through five were summarized at the beginning of chapter six). In doing so, we will review
a number of the "moves" we have considered that help "set us up"
for this synchronistic recognition, especially some that may help
when we feel we have lost our connection with open awareness.

SUMMARY, CHAPTERS SIX THROUGH TEN

In chapter six, "Motivation and Effortlessness," we considered the style with which we approach this work, particularly the delicate nature of our approach to methods and practices. We reflected on the motivation we might have for seeking realization, the double-edged sword of "a gaining idea" and of longing for union with the Beloved. We saw that the least entangling motivation for doing this work is simply *because we have to*, "because," to quote from that chapter, "we are inseparable from the awakening of life to itself. We do this for the sake of everything — which includes our loved ones, children yet to be born, all who suffer, everyone. We do it for the sake of this beautiful world....The most reliable motivation — if we need one — that helps our heart open when we feel ourselves contracting, is this desire to awaken for the sake of others."

In chapter seven we turned to the question of prayer and its seeming conflict with realizing nondual awareness. Acknowledging the dualistic nature of much religious expression and prayer, we recognized how prayer can nevertheless serve as a bridge that is accessible to us in our journey "toward the One." We considered the several forms of prayer — prayers of petition, invocatory prayer, spontaneous prayer, liturgical prayer, prayers of approach and nearness, and their benefits and limitations. Since praying in one form or another arises naturally for many of us, how can we learn to pray wisely so that we do not inadvertently reinforce a dualistic mindset? We reflected on what it means to be "good translators," allowing the words of our prayers to open beyond their literal meanings to the essence they seek to represent. And we contemplated the intent of prayers of identity and prayers of silence, in which awareness of "God within is awakened and made living."

Chapter eight described "The Art of Awakening," an art that calls upon our spontaneous and direct engagement with perception. In it we reviewed the familiar sense that "something is missing," and the paradox of spiritual practice in aid of realization versus the recognition that nothing we do will result in the realization we wish for. In the context of this paradox we considered the art of awakening and forms of its practice, specifically: *conversations that release, developing a non-doing contemplative practice,* and the "practice" of *release at inception.* The essential point of this chapter was to encourage you to become "your own creative artist of awakening — curious, experimental, and honest."

In chapter nine, "A Joyous Cosmology," we dived into a series of contemplations inspired by early Dzogchen teachings, exploring the nature of *absence, openness, spontaneity, and oneness* as they touch our most intimate sense of being. Within these contemplations we considered once again the ways in which thoughts, feelings, and perceptions of "the real world" arise and vanish in our awareness; the ineffable nature of awareness itself; and our experience of the "face" of absence or emptiness. Here we also came to appreciate how *opening into openness* is the essence of our work, and the intimacy of being a *clearing* in which the world gathers. Finally, we touched for a moment the mystery of universal, timeless spontaneity and *wahdat al wujud,* the Oneness of Being.

Chapter ten, "The Ocean of Kindness," turned to discovering a reliable basis for our actions in the world. We were guided in this by looking through the lens of our own present-moment experience as we explored the possibility of nondual action (*wei wu wei*) and the still point of equanimity — equanimity being "the necessary ease within which appropriate action is possible." Lastly, after all our contemplations of absence, nothingness, openness, and the ineffable, we attempted to "break through any complacency we might have that we actually know what the mystery is that we call the One." Allowing it to be beyond our knowing, we considered the possibility that it — the mystery of Being — is, in Longchenpa's words, "wholly positive," in Inayat Khan's words, "the perfection of love," in Garab Dorje's words, "the All-Good." This "basic goodness" (Trungpa Rinpoche's words) appears in our realization as a fundamental tendency toward kindness — "done on the spot without any thought of kindness."

THE HEART OF THE MATTER

Near the end of his life, Inayat Khan gave a talk on the relationship between spirit and matter. The talk concluded with these words:

> *What is consciousness?*
> *Consciousness is the knowing faculty,*
> *but it is the knowing faculty when it has some knowledge —*
> *it is only then that we call it consciousness.*
> *One is conscious of something,*
> *consciousness must always be conscious of something.*
> *When consciousness is not conscious of anything*
> *it is pure intelligence.*
> *It is in this realization that the greatest secret of life can be*
>   *revealed.*
>
> *One might say that the experience of pure intelligence*
> *is possible only for the only Being, for God,*
> *but no one can stand outside of the only Being.*
> *The only Being includes all.*
>
> *And undoubtedly there is a certain process*
> *by which one can attain to this pure intelligence.*
> *Man is not conscious of it anymore —*
> *he has lost the habit of experiencing what pure intelligence is.*
> *But all the meditations and concentrations,*

*the whole process by which the mystic treads the spiritual path
brings us finally to the realization of that pure intelligence.*

*If one asks what benefit one derives from it,
the answer is that since all that benefits us
comes from one source, that source must be perfect.
It must be all-beneficial.
It is beyond our limited imagination,
but it is the greatest thing one can attain in one's life.*[42]

These words point directly to the central purpose of the Open Path: realization of the "pure intelligence" (in our words, *pure open awareness*) that is the greatest "secret" of life. Inayat Khan speaks of "the whole process by which the mystic treads the spiritual path" — the meditations and concentrations — as dedicated to this fundamental realization of pure awareness.

As we know by now, whatever "process" we follow to attain realization — no matter how subtle — walks a very fine line between serving our realization and serving, in Keith Dowman's words, "the anxiety entailed by prostituting the moment for some future benefit." The very idea of creating a guide to the Open Path like this book, and of following it as we have done, could be criticized for its tendency to detour us in this way — fixing our hopes and efforts on the promise of realization to come. And yet, as we also know, there are clear and obvious benefits to practices that help us to calm our mind, open our heart, and release our identification with our history of fixations.

I repeat this paradox here so that we are aware in the present moment of our tendency to look to "some future benefit" when we consider the idea of realization. *Realization?* we ask. *Am I realized now? Have I attained it?* We look around in our present-moment experience: *where is realization? I don't see anything special. I must not be realized.*

Uh oh! Is everyone else realized except me? How would I know if I am? What can I do to hurry up and attain realization?

Questions like these are beautiful. They seem to stop us in our tracks. They hang awkwardly in the moment, surrounded by silence. When we look closely at them they begin to reveal how we assume ourselves to be entities that are located somewhere, a location that can either be described by this idea called realization or by its lack. Thus in our imagination the idea of realization that is at the center of these questions is also *located* somewhere: either here, now (in space and time), or somewhere else in space and time.

As we notice this spatial and temporal basis of our idea of realization, we see how we are indeed "prostituting the moment" for the promise of some future benefit. We are selling out this moment now by asserting that something is missing (that is, realization) — it is somewhere else. In so doing we are missing the present as well as conditioning the future.

Seeing this plainly, a kind of inner sigh arises from us at the impossibility of our predicament: we may not *feel* ourselves to be realized now, but that very feeling is the main impediment to our realization!

At this moment, not having any alternative, it may happen that we simply give up. We stop trying to find realization. We stop trying altogether. There's nothing we can do. And, after all, there doesn't seem to be anyone to do it, even if there might be something to be done.

Reading this, or going through a similar process a few hours from now, we might look up from this page or from the middle of what we're doing and simply notice what *is* — what is without our commentary or interpretations. *"Is?" What does that mean?* The shapes and colors, sounds and sensations of our environment are present as always, but when we look closely we see even these *apparently existing* phenomena waver and shift in our awareness moment by moment.

I can't really say that any of these things "is" since they keep changing, at least in my perception of them, which is all I really can be sure of. So what "is" that is not wavering or shifting?

If we stop now in the flow of our thoughts and simply wait to see if we can discern what is not wavering and shifting, we may notice what could be described as a "transparent openness" — although to say we notice it may be misleading because it doesn't appear as anything at all. It has no characteristics, except that it seems to be congruent with both awareness itself and the present instant, and it doesn't seem to have any spatial location. It completely penetrates what we have thought of as *inside* and *outside*. And it is somehow a vast quietness — the epitome of silence itself — yet the sounds of our environment don't stop.

Now if we shout, *I've got it! Realization!*, we observe that those words appear and vanish without doing anything. No one *has* anything. Nothing changed. "Realization" is neither more nor less here than it has always been. *But it's so simple! There's nothing here!*

The "nothing" that is here is simultaneously the entire, vast creation. As Longchenpa describes it:

> *Within the expanse of spontaneous presence*
> *is the ground for all that arises.*
> *Empty in essence, continuous by nature,*
> *it has never existed as anything whatsoever,*
> *yet arises as anything at all.*[43]

If you have followed this narrative so far, you will recognize that the heart of the matter is simply direct perception in the timeless moment of the here-and-now, without any evaluation of a perceiver or a world perceived. Everything is resolved *now*. Any thoughts of realization and getting it or not getting it are just that — thoughts.

In this moment, and this, and this, we don't have to do anything, or practice anything, or improve, or move toward any dimension other than *this, now.* In fact, what could move? As Inayat Khan reminds us, "No one can stand outside of the only Being." This is the heart of the matter. No one is in control. This transparent, silent, pure intelligence is it, though it has never existed as anything whatsoever!

FALLING FROM HEAVEN

The preceding section tracks one of the innumerable ways we can "talk ourselves into" realization. Like all clusters of words, the words above are approximate and have a limited shelf-life. As we recognized in chapter eight, "The Art of Awakening," our job is to continually refresh these kinds of contemplations — whether they are verbal like this one or are experienced more kinesthetically and intuitively — so that we can see through the accumulation of our opinions and simply rest in the openness of the moment.

And yet it happens that no matter how clearly we may have experienced the lucid presence of open awareness, there comes a time when we feel we have "lost it." Mundane reality stubbornly resumes its hold on our perceptions, and we sense ourselves isolated and identified in the old way. It may be that we have gotten attached to an outcome of a task, or have had a disagreement with someone, or have become a little anxious about what might happen in the future, and then...gone, gone, gone my enlightenment! We have fallen from heaven.

How shall we be with this? What can we do? How shall we find it again? This is one of the most familiar issues that come up for all of us as we proceed on the path. While I have addressed this experience a number of times throughout this book, I'd like to summarize here a few of the reminders that may be helpful when we realize we have "lost it."

1. DO NOTHING

Probably the most understandable reaction we have when we feel we have "lost it" is to look for it. After all, we do this when we lose anything, like our car keys. We look for them! How else could we find them? Here it is helpful to remember that the "realization" we are looking for is not a thing like our car keys. Rather, it: (1) is invisible; (2) has no marks or contours; (3) has no location; (4) does not appear as anything at all; and (5) cannot be found by looking for it. It does not and will not arrive as a result of anything we might do or strive for.

These kinds of reminders help to frustrate the acquisitive tendency of our mind. Since we don't know what to do, and in any case doing something would be useless, we simply stop doing anything. This "stop" is essential. In itself it is not a "doing" since it is the cessation of doing. It doesn't take any effort. We just relax, present to what is. No commentary necessary. We take it easy. We may become aware of how our mind tries to reassert a "me" and an "other" — by thinking about realization, or doubting our ability, or distracting our self in some other way. But we just notice these movements without response. We stay "stopped," doing nothing.

In the emptiness of this stop, we recognize that "realization" is already here. In fact, we see *there is no realization*. "It" — whatever it is — is empty of being anything. It is this timeless moment, perfectly pure, pristine, and everywhere. It is transparently present like space itself.

2. NO NEED TO KNOW

Another response to the sense of having "lost it" is to recognize that the idea "I have lost it" is a thought. As a thought it can't help but reify into an "it" (some sort of object, even if only a conceptual one) whatever it is we feel we have lost. By asserting to ourselves that we have lost it we are also asserting that we know what it is. But this that we're talking about can't be known. It is, after all, *not a thought, a thing, or a feeling of any kind.* The mind can't touch it and never will.

Reminding ourselves of this fact brings us to the same stop mentioned above in relation to our wanting to do something to make heaven come back. But the habit of wanting to know is even more insistent than the habit of wanting to do. This is not surprising — our education throughout life has engrained in us the importance of knowing things. In many realms this is quite logical, but in recognizing the open awareness that is the ground of all being, thinking we need to know *what it is* just gets in our way.

When the possessive nature of the need to know is gone, what is left? See if you can experience this directly, now. Allow yourself to no longer need to know what this sentence is about, or this paragraph, or this chapter, or the Open Path, or anything. For this moment at least, see if you can relax the acquisitiveness of your mind. No need to figure out anything. If you can relax like this and still read this sentence, that's fine; if not, experiment while not reading and then come back to reading later.

When the need to know is relaxed, perhaps you will notice a kind of clear-headedness, a freshness, that isn't exactly a sensation but more like a relief — like the absence of a pressure that used to be there. While this clear-headedness can't be produced by something you do or think, it becomes evident when the *neediness* of needing to know is released.

Clear-headedness is a way of describing the recognition of clear, contentless, open awareness. Rest in this clear-headedness. It is also clear-heartedness. Rest here — it is free! Nothing to do, nothing to know, nothing to figure out, nothing to improve. It is the ever-fresh moment, without any need to grasp it or manipulate it.

3. NO SUBJECT

Another direct response to the feeling of "I am lost" or "I have lost it" is simply to turn around and notice that this construction privileges the "I." What is it that has lost open awareness? Be careful here, since we have learned this inquiry early on and it can easily become just a repetitive game rather than a profound inquiry. Let yourself be present to the unfindability of yourself (which admittedly is an odd way to say it!). In Jean Klein's words, "Get to know those moments when you are nothing."

You can substitute any subject-centered thoughts or feelings here if they are present to you, such as "I am bored," or "I am lonely," or "I don't get this," or "I am depressed." What is it that is depressed? What is it that is lonely? If the response is "me!" notice how that sense of "me" is actually an *object* in your awareness. The typical thing we call a *subject* — the me — is actually a shifting constellation of thoughts (reflections) that are interpreted as evidence of an internal entity called "me." What is the real subject? What is aware of the feeling or thought of me? Who is being described? What are you really?

By now you are familiar with this turn, and will notice quickly that whatever you really are is not perceivable by your mind. So relax. Whatever it is that feels it has "lost it" is unfindable. In this recognition *all* fixations and constructions erode away, since they have no place to dwell.

4. LISTENING TO LISTENING

Let us also remember here the simple guidance we focused on early in this book: start where you are. Accept what is. Listen to what is arising. (You might recall here the line from Longchenpa in chapter nine: *Whatever occurs, whatever it may be, that itself is the key....*) So if you are experiencing the sense of having "lost it," you can start with that. What exactly is arising that signifies for you this loss? Is it a thought? A feeling? Whatever it is, let it be in your awareness without elaborating on it. Notice that no matter how intensely the sense of loss may appear, after a period of time it is replaced by a different feeling or series of thoughts. So you let that be. You "listen" dispassionately, unattached to what comes up. At a certain point the shifting objects — the thoughts, feelings, and sensations — appearing in your awareness lose their interest for you, and you relax into the listening itself.

This dynamic is what Jean Klein speaks of as "listening to listening," a process of listening that moves from a focus on the content of what arises to the capacity of listening itself. In the following passage he describes this succinctly:

> To discover your innermost being you must start from where you are at this very moment, wherever that is. You cannot begin anywhere else. Whatever appears before you — your body, sensations, feelings, thoughts, etc. — must be accepted, listened to as a whole. This does not mean you should analyze, interpret, understand or look for an inner meaning. What is important is to discover listening itself, which sooner or later will be revealed to you. At first the accent is on what is listened to, the sensation, feeling or thought. But the more the listening is sustained the more emphasis is shifted to this listening itself without a listened to. Then you are at the threshold of the source from which the listening derives. That very instant listening will become a living reality. [44]

5. POINTINGS

Sometimes all that is needed when we feel separated from recognizing the transparent ground of open awareness is to open a book of nondual teachings and read a few lines. Perhaps a poem or part of an old scripture will serve. Perhaps a simple word like "spaciousness" will do it, or a practice like the practice of subtle opening. Keep it simple. It may be that all you need to do is walk alone in nature and experience your oneness with its pure intelligence. Or you may be fortunate enough to have a good friend who also has experience with nondual realization. As you express to him or her your sense of being out of touch, you may receive the most relevant guidance or encouragement, or through sharing the communion of silence together. However, you need to be careful when in conversation with others while you are feeling lost and vulnerable. You may receive a lot of well-meaning advice that ends up only making you feel insecure or conflicted. There is a difference between *a pointing out* and *a point of view*. Points of view tend to be fixed and assertive. A pointing out is always open-ended, like the koan question "what is this?" and does not create separation or give you more to think about. It gestures to nothing, and is "on your side" so to speak, recognizing that what you feel you have lost has already been returned to you, and in fact it never left.

6. RELAX

Finally, if you feel you have "lost it," be at ease. You can be sure as dawn follows night that realization of pure, open awareness will return. You can absolutely trust that. It is the natural condition of your being and of all being. Actually you know already that it can't go anywhere, so it can neither return *nor* be lost. No need to spend energy being concerned that you've lost it. The ground of all being cannot be lost. Know that simply by opening yourself to "it" again and again, in all these ways, your capacity to sustain its natural presence throughout your daily life will increase.

THE INVISIBLE OFFERING

As we come to the end of our journey together, I would like to mention a dynamic that, while perhaps unspoken, has been present with us throughout this introduction to the Open Path. Let us call it *the invisible offering*. It is not complicated — these words simply refer to *your participation in the natural gift of awakening*. Your dedication to exploring the Open Path is an aspect of this gift. Your engagement with this book, and in hundreds of conversations, in being curious, in sharing inquiry, in helping others to understand something, in sitting alone in contemplation, all these are aspects of this gift. Your realization itself is the heart of this gift, both to your own life and to all the life that your life touches. *It is in this realization that the greatest secret of life can be revealed.*

To call it a gift or an offering is to say that the awakening you have come to realize *gives of itself.* It isn't a private attainment. The openness of the Open Path can be described in many ways, one of which is its natural, open generosity. It is an invisible offering given to us and through us. No credit is due anyone. It simply gives of itself. Perhaps this is one way to speak of the innate quality I called in the previous chapter "the ocean of kindness." It gives of itself.

A simple principle: *if you wish to deepen your realization, give it.* Be it. Let it offer itself through you. This doesn't necessarily mean that you have to teach others, or try to explain the spontaneous presence of open awareness, or share your experiences with them, although this might very well happen. "Letting your realization offer itself through you" fundamentally means resting in it as often and as naturally as possible, and allowing "its" presence to do the rest. It is naturally patient, compassionate, unencumbered, and at ease. It is present and unopinionated and responsive. It is dignified and care-free.

This dynamic of "invisible offering" is like a sacred current — a continuous initiation that we have opened our lives to. Perhaps we could also call it the current of transmission. But we don't have to get too complicated with our thoughts about it — all that is implied here is that we recognize the invisible beauty of this current and let it flow through us however it will.

> *Give a gift to your brother, but there's no gift*
> *to compare with the assurance that he*
> *is the golden eternity. The true understanding of*
> *this would bring tears to your eyes.*
> *The other shore is right here...*[45]

—JACK KEROUAC

Notes

1. Sri Nisargadatta Maharaj, I Am That: Talks with Sri Nisargadatta Maharaj. Translated by Maurice Frydman, Durham, NC: The Acorn Press, 2005, p. 241. (Ms.) Indu Rastogi. Business Manager The Acorn Press, Durham, NC 27715-3279.

2. In this passage from Ibn Al 'Arabi I have taken the liberty of changing the personal pronoun "You" that appears in the original text — a typical way Sufis address God or Allah — to the impersonal words "This" and "It." These words signify unconditioned, open, self-occurring awareness, the ground of being, Buddha-nature, etc., just as the word "You" does for Sufis and other mystics who are comfortable with the intimacy implicit in this kind of personalization. However, in the quotations from Sufis and others that occur in the rest of this book I leave these words — "You," "Thee," "God," "Lord," "Allah," "He," "Him," "Beloved," "Friend," etc., — as they appear in the original texts, and encourage those readers who are not comfortable with this kind of personalization to simply translate them to "This," "It," or any other signifier you prefer for this that we are speaking of: the spontaneous presence of the ground of being that is ultimately and always unnamable.

Here is the original translation of the Ibn Al 'Arabi text:

How can I know You when You are the Inwardly Hidden who is not known?

How Can I not know You when You are the Outwardly Manifest, making Yourself known to me in everything?

How can I realise Your Unity when in Uniqueness I have no existence?

How can I not realise Your Unity when Union is the very secret of servanthood?

Glory be to You! There is no god but You! No-one but You can realise Your Unity, for You are as You are in pre-eternity without beginning and post-eternity without end. In reality, no other than You can realise Your Unity, and in sum, none knows You except You.

You hide and You manifest — yet You do not hide from Yourself nor do you manifest to other than Yourself, for You are You. There is no god but You. How is this paradox to be resolved, when the First is Last and the Last is First?

From: *Muhyiddin Ibn 'Arabi, Seven Days of the Heart: Prayers for the Nights and Days of the Week* (Oxford, UK: Anqa Publishing, 2000), 43-44.

3. Jelalludin Rumi, *The Essential Rumi.*(San Francisco, CA: Harper-One, 2004), 168.

4. Muhyiddin Ibn Al 'Arabi, *What the Seeker Needs* (VT: Threshold Books, 1992), 31.

5. Inayat Khan, *The Dance of the Soul: Gayan, Vadan, Nirtan* (New Delhi, India: Motilal Banadsidass, 2008), "Saum."

6. Tsoknyi Rinpoche, *Carefree Dignity: Discourses on Training in the Nature of Mind* (Berkeley, CA: North Atlantic Books, 2004).

7. Longchenpa, *The Precious Treasury of the Way of Abiding* (Junction City, CA: Padma, 1998), 174.

8. Sri Nisargadatta Maharaj, *I Am That: Talks with Sri Nisargadatta Maharaj.* Translated by Maurice Frydman, Durham, NC: The Acorn Press, 2005, p. 241. (Ms.) Indu Rastogi. Business Manager The Acorn Press, Durham, NC 27715-3279.

9. David Loy, "Avoiding the Void: The Lack of Self in Psychotherapy and Buddhism," Journal of Transpersonal Psychology, vol. 24, no. 2, p. 176 (1992).

10. Jean Klein, *The Ease of Being* (Durham, NC: The Acorn Press), 99.

11. Indeep Media, Michael Courtney, "Science vs Philosophy, Forethought and Free Will," indeepmedia.wordpress.com/2011/09/15/science-vs-philosophy-forethought-and-free-will/

12. Wei Wu Wei, *Why Lazurus Laughed* (Boulder, CO: Sentient Publications, 2003), 80.

13. Michael Sells, *Early Islamic Mysticism* (Mahwah, NJ: Paulist Press, 1995).

14. Ibn Al 'Arabi, *What the Seeker Needs*, 39.

15. Jean Klein, *Be Who You Are*, translated by Mary Mann. Copyright © Non-Duality Press August 2006 & 2007 Coyright © Emma Edwards ISBN: 978-0-9551762-5-8 (Salisbury, UK: Non-Duality Press, 2006), 9-10.

16. Peter Fenner, *Radiant Mind* (Boulder, CO: Sounds True, 2007), 88.

17. Longchenpa, *Natural Perfection,* © Keith Dowman, 2010. Reprinted from *Natural Perfection: Longchenpa's Radical Dzogchen* with permission from Wisdom Publications, 199 Elm Street, Somerville, MA 02144 USA, p. 107. www.wisdompubs.org.

18. Longchenpa, *Natural Perfection,* 23.

19. Rumi, *The Essential Rumi,* 112.

20. Jelalludin Rumi, *The Soul of Rumi* (San Francisco, CA: HarperOne, 2002) 96.

21. Rumi, *The Essential Rumi,* 155.

22. From the Penguin publication *I Heard God Laughing, Poems of Hope and Joy, Renderings of Hafiz,* copyright 1996 & 2006 Daniel Landinsky, and used with his permission.

23. Rumi, *The Essential Rumi,* 13.

24. Inayat Khan, *The Dance of the Soul: Gayan, Vadan, Nirtan.* New Delhi, India: Motilal Banarsidass, 2008.

25. Khan, *The Dance of the Soul, (Khatoum).*

26. Shabkar Lama, *The Flight of the Garuda,* © Keith Dowman, 2003. Reprinted from *The Flight of the Garuda* with permission from Wisdom Publications, 199 Elm Street, Somerville, MA 02144 USA, p. 118. www.wisdompubs.org.

27. Root sources of Chapter 9:
Longchenpa (Dowman translation). *Natural Perfection.* (Somerville, MA: Wisdom Publications, 2010).

———— (Richard Barron translation). *The Precious Treasury of the Way of Abiding.* (Junction City, CA: Padma, 1998).

Norbu, Chogyal Namkhai, and Adriano Clemente (translators). *The Supreme Source: The Fundamental Tantra of Dzogchen Semde* (Ithaca, NY: Snow Lion Publications, 1999).

28. Ibn Al 'Arabi, *What the Seeker Needs,* 40.

29. Rumi, *The Essential Rumi,* 272.

30. Longchenpa, *Natural Perfection,* 261.

31. Rumi, *The Essential Rumi,* 105.

32. Wallace Stevens, "Final Soliloquy of the Internal Paramour," *The Collected Poems of Wallace Stevens* (New York, NY: Vintage, 1990).

33. By Thomas Merton, from THE WAY OF CHUANG TZU, copyright © 1965 by The Abbey of Gethsemeni. Reprinted by permission of New Directions Publishing Corp.

34. Koun Yamada, *Gateless Gate* (Los Angeles, CA: Center Publications, 1979), 86.

35. By Thomas Merton, from THE WAY OF CHUANG TZU, copyright © 1965 by The Abbey of Gethsemeni. Reprinted by permission of New Directions Publishing Corp.

36. T.S. Eliot, *The Four Quartets, "Burnt Norton"* (Mariner Books, 1968).

37. Stephen Batchelor, *Buddhism Without Beliefs: A Contemporary Guide to Awakening* (New York, NY: Riverhead Books, 1998), 80.

38. Longchenpa (Richard Barron translation), *The Precious Treasury of the Basic Space of Phenomena* (Junction City, CA: Padma, 1998), 9.

39. Jack Kerouac, *The Scripture of the Golden Eternity,* Copyright © 1994 by Jan Kerouac and Anthony Sampatakakos (San Francisco, CA: City Lights, 2001), 34.

40. Kerouac, 53.

41. I am indebted to Stephen Batchelor and Joanna Macy for inspiring this exercise.

42. Inayat Khan, *The Sufi Message, vol. 11, Philosophy, Psychology, and Mysticism* (New Delhi, India: Motilal Banadsidass, 2011).

43. Longchenpa, *The Precious Treasury of the Basic Space of Phenomena,* 3.

44. Jean Klein, *I Am,* Copyright © Non-Duality Press August 2006 & 2007, Copyright © Emma Edwards ISBN: 978-0-9551762-7-2 (Salisbury, UK: Non-Duality Press, 2006), 116.

45. Kerouac, 40.

Bibliography

I recommend any of the following books for those who wish to pursue the study of nondual teachings through different traditions.

Adamson, Sailor Bob, and Wheeler, John. *Presence-Awareness.* Salisbury, UK: Non-Duality Press, 2004.

————. *What's Wrong with Right Now?* Salisbury, UK: Non-Duality Press, 2004.

Adyashanti. *Emptiness Dancing.* Boulder, CO: Sounds True, 2006.

————. *Falling into Grace.* Boulder, CO: Sounds True, 2011.

Bailey, Darryl. *Dismantling the Fantasy.* Salisbury, UK: Non-Duality Press, 2010.

Balsekar, Ramesh. *A Net of Jewels.* Hermosa Beach, CA: Advaita Press, 1996.

Batchelor, Stephen. *Buddhism Without Beliefs: A Contemporary Guide to Awakening.* New York, NY: Riverhead Books, 1998.

Beck, Charlotte Joko. *Nothing Special: Living Zen.* San Francisco, CA: HarperOne, 1994.

Carse, David. *Perfect Brilliant Stillness.* Shelburne, VT: Paragate Publishing, 2005.

Chuang Tzu (translated by Thomas Merton). *The Way of Chuang Tzu.* New York, NY: New Directions, 2010.

Dowman, Keith. *Eye of the Storm: Vairotsana's Five Original Transmissions.* Kathmandu, Nepal: Vajra Publications, 2006.

————. and Longchenpa. *Maya Yoga.* Kathmandu, Nepal: Vajra Publications, 2010.

Dziuban, Peter Francis. *Consciousness Is All: Now Life Is Completely New.* Nevada City, CA: Blue Dolphin Publishing, 2006.

Ernst, Carl. *Words of Ecstasy in Sufism.* Albany, NY: SUNY, 1985.

Fenner, Peter. *Radiant Mind.* Boulder, CO: Sounds True, 2007.

Gangaji. *The Diamond in Your Pocket.* Boulder, CO: Sounds True, 2007.

Hafiz, translated by Daniel Landinsky. *The Gift.* New York, NY: Penguin Compass, 1999.

———. *The Subject Tonight Is Love.* New York, NY: Penguin, 2003.

———. *I Heard God Laughing.* New York, NY: Penguin, 2006.

Harding, Douglas. *On Having No Head: Zen and the Rediscovery of the Obvious.* Vista, CA: Inner Directions, 2002.

———. *Face to No-Face.* Vista, CA: Inner Directions, 2000.

Hartong, Leo. *From Self to Self.* Salisbury, UK: Non-Duality Press, 2005.

———. *Awakening to the Dream: The Gift of Lucid Living.* Salisbury, UK: Non-Duality Press, 2003.

Heidegger, Martin. *Conversation on a Country Path about Thinking,* in *Discourse on Thinking.* New York, NY: Harper Perennial, 1969.

Hixon, Lex. *Coming Home: The Experience of Enlightenment in Sacred Traditions.* Burdett, NY: Larson Publications, 1995.

———. *Mother of the Buddhas: Meditations on the Prajnaparamita Sutra.* Wheaton, IL: Quest Books, 1993.

Ibn Al 'Arabi. Muhyiddin. *The Bezels of Wisdom.* Mahwah, NJ: Paulist Press, 1980.

———. *Journey to the Lord of Power.* Rochester, VT: Inner Traditions, 1981.

———. and Chittick, William. *The Self-Disclosure of God.* Albany, NY: SUNY, 1997.

———. *What the Seeker Needs.* VT: Threshold Books, 1992.

———. (translated by Pablo Beneito and Stephen Hirtenstein). *Seven Days of the Heart: Prayers for the Nights and Days of the Week.* Oxford, UK: Anqa Publishing, 2000.

Kabir, versions by Robert Bly. *Ecstatic Poems.* Boston, MA: Beacon Press, 2007.

Katie, Byron, with Mitchell, Stephen. *A Thousand Names for Joy.* New York, NY: Three Rivers Press, 2008.

Kerouac, Jack. *The Scripture of the Golden Eternity.* San Francisco, CA: City Lights, 2001.

Khan, Inayat. *The Sufi Message: 14 Volume Set.* New Delhi, India: Motilal Banadsidass, 2011. (Many single volumes also available through Omega Publications.)

———. *The Dance of the Soul: Gayan, Vadan, Nirtan.* New Delhi, India: Motilal Banadsidass, 2008.

Klein, Jean. *Who Am I?* UK: Element Books, 1991.

———. *Be Who You Are.* Salisbury, UK: Non-Duality Press, 2006.

———. *Beyond Knowledge.* Salisbury, UK: Non-Duality Press, 2006.

———. *I Am.* Salisbury, UK: Non-Duality Press, 2006.

———. *The Ease of Being.* Durham, NC: Acorn Press, 1986

———. *Transmission of the Flame.* London and Santa Barbara: Third Millennium Publications, 1991.

———. *Living Truth.* Salisbury, UK: Non-Duality Press, 2007.

Longchenpa (Dowman translation). *Natural Perfection.* Somerville, MA: Wisdom Publications, 2010.

———. (Dowman translation). *Maya Yoga.* Kathmandu, Nepal: Vajra Publications, 2010.

———. (Richard Barron translation). *The Precious Treasury of the Way of Abiding.* Junction City, CA: Padma, 1998

———. (Richard Barron translation). *The Precious Treasury of the Basic Space of Phenomena.* Junction City, CA: Padma, 1998

———. (Richard Barron translation). *A Treasure Trove of Scriptural Transmission: A Commentary on The Precious Treasury of the Basic Space of Phenomena.* Junction City, CA: Padma, 1998.

Loy, David. *Lack and Transcendence: The Problem of Death and Life in Psychotherapy, Existentialism, and Buddhism.* Amherst, NY: Prometheus Books/Humanity Books, 2001.

———. *Nonduality.* Amherst, NY: Humanity Books, 1997.

Lucille, Francis. *Eternity Now.* Salisbury, UK: Non-Duality Press, 2008.

———. *The Perfume of Silence.* Temecula, CA: Truespeech Productions, 2006.

Nagarjuna (Translated by Stephen Batchelor). *Verses from the Center: A Buddhist Vision of the Sublime.* New York, NY: Riverhead Books, 2000.

Liquorman, Wayne. *Never Mind: A Journey into Nonduality.* Hermosa Beach, CA: Advaita Press, 2004.

Nisargadatta Maharaj. *I Am That.* NC: Acorn Press, 1990

———. *The Experience of Nothingness: Talks on Realizing the Infinite.* San Diego, CA: Blue Dove Press, 1996.

Maharshi, Ramana (ed. by Arthur Osborne). *The Collected Works of Ramana Maharshi.* Tiruvannamalai, India: Sri Ramnasramam, 2009.

Merrell-Wolff. *Franklin Merrell-Wolff's Experience and Philosophy: A Personal Record of Transformation and a Discussion of Transcendental Consciousness.* Albany, NY: SUNY, 1994.

Namgyal, Dakpo Tashi (translated by Eric Pema Kunsang and Khenchen Thrangu Rinpoche). *Clarifying the Natural State.* Berkeley, CA: North Atlantic Books, 2004.

Norbu, Chogyal Namkhai, and Adriano Clemente. *The Supreme Source: The Fundamental Tantra of Dzogchen Semde*. Ithaca, NY: Snow Lion Publications, 1999.

Parsons, Tony. *Invitation to Awaken: Embracing Our Natural State of Presence*. Carlsbad, CA: Inner Directions, 2004.

———. *As It Is: The Open Secret of Spiritual Awakening*. Carlsbad, CA: Inner Directions, 2000.

Pendergrast, John, Peter Fenner, and Sheila Krystal, eds. *The Sacred Mirror: Nondual Wisdom and Psychotherapy*. St. Paul, MN: Paragon House, 2003.

———. and Kenneth Bradford, eds. *Listening from the Heart of Silence (second volume of Nondual Wisdom and Psychotherapy)*. St. Paul, MN: Paragon House, 2007.

Rumi, Jelalludin (versions by Coleman Barks). *The Essential Rumi*. San Francisco, CA: HarperOne, 2004.

———. *The Glance: Songs of Soul Meeting*. New York, NY: Penguin, 2001.

———. *The Book of Love: Poems of Ecstasy and Longing*. San Francisco, CA: HarperOne, 2003.

———. *The Soul of Rumi*. San Francisco, CA: HarperOne, 2002.

———. *The Big Red Book*. San Francisco, CA: HarperOne, 2011.

Schuon, Frithjof. *Sufism – Veil and Quintessence*. Bloomington, IN: World Wisdom, 2006

———. *The Transcendent Unity of Religions*. Wheaton, IL: Quest Books, 1984.

Sells, Michael. *Mystical Languages of Unsaying*. Chicago, IL: University of Chicago Press, 1994.

———. *Early Islamic Mysticism*. Mahwah, NJ: Paulist Press, 1995.

Shabkar Lama (translated by Keith Dowman). *The Flight of the Garuda*. Somerville, MA: Wisdom Publications, 1994.

Spira, Rupert. *The Transparency of Things*. Salisbury, UK: Non-Duality Press, 2008.

———. *Presence: The Intimacy of All Experience, Vols. I & II*. Salisbury, UK: Non-Duality Press, 2011.

Tarrant, John. *Bring Me the Rhinoceros*. Boston, MA: Shambhala, 2008.

Tolle, Eckhart. *The Power of Now*. Novato, CA: New World Library, 2004.

———. *A New Earth*. New York, NY: Penguin, 2008.

Tolifson, Joan. *Awake in the Heartland: The Ecstasy of What Is*. Salisbury, UK: Non-Duality Press, 2006.

Tsoknyi Rinpoche. *Carefree Dignity: Discourses on Training in the Nature of Mind*. Berkeley, CA: North Atlantic Books, 2004.

———. *Fearless Simplicity: The Dzogchen Way of Living Freely in a Complex World*. Berkeley, CA: North Atlantic Books, 2004.

Wei Wu Wei. *Fingers Pointing to the Moon: Reflections of a Pilgrim on the Way*. Boulder, CO: Sentient Publications, 2003.

———. *Why Lazarus Laughed: The Essential Doctrine, Zen—Advaita—Tantra.* . Boulder, CO: Sentient Publications, 2003.

Welwood, John. *Toward a Psychology of Awakening*. Boston, MA: Shambhala, 2002.

Wheeler, John. *Awakening to the Natural State*. Salisbury, UK: Non-Duality Press, 2004.

———. *Right Here, Right Now*. Salisbury, UK: Non-Duality Press, 2006.

———. *Shining in Plain View*. Salisbury, UK: Non-Duality Press, 2005.

Gratitude to Teachers and Sources

The Open Path as expressed in this book borrows freely from the wisdom, language, and methods of a long list of teachers. Some of these men and women I have worked with directly, others I have studied through their writings. I'd like to acknowledge here my debt to them.

In the realm of Sufis, my spiritual path has been of course deeply influenced by Sufi Inayat Khan, the scope of his vision, its generosity and beauty, and its basis in nondual realization. My long relationship as a student of Pir-o-Murshid Fazal Inayat-Khan was most crucial for the unfoldment of this work, especially the influence of his mystic vision and articulation, his insight into psychological-spiritual dynamics, his music, and his gift for experiential education. Murshida Shahzadi Khan-de-Konig and Pir-o-Murshida Sitara Brutnell were also profound teachers and exemplars for me. Shaykh Ahmed Kostas of the Qadiri Order in Fez opened me to the mysticism of Islam and to the power of zikr practice. Of course among the classical Sufis I owe an immense debt to the nondual wisdom evident in the writings of Niffari, Jelaluddin Rumi, Hafiz, Kabir, and Ibn 'Arabi in particular.

Turning to my Buddhist mentors: Joanna Macy was an important teacher and friend — her accessible teachings revealed the meaning of non-self, and her skill with experiential exercises was a priceless teaching. Roshi Joan Halifax both taught me a mystical activism and welcomed me into the Lineage of the Matriarchs of the White Plum Sangha of the Soto Zen tradition. Achaan Sulak Sivaraksa, Thai Buddhist activist, teacher, and friend, was a formidable influence on my teaching and activism for over fifteen years. The Buddhist author David Loy has also influenced my understanding of the dynamics of the ego.

In the realm of Christian mystics I have been profoundly touched by the example of Father Paolo Dall'Oglio of the Monastery of St. Moses in Syria, and the writings of the Hesychast tradition, which advance a Christian mysticism. In addition, I have been influenced by the work of the Christian Sufi Fritjof Schuon. From the Jewish tradition I have been guided by the teachings and friendship of Rabbi Zalman Schachter-Shalomi.

I am thankful for the essentially nondual teachings I received over several years from William and Spotted Eagle, roadmen of the Native American Church and the Assemblies of the Morning Star. In the same vein, the many years of rites-of-passage teachings I received from my dear friends Steven and Meredith Foster in the deserts of southern California taught me about death and transformation.

In the expanding field of nondual teaching, I am most indebted to my friend and teacher Peter Fenner, a former Tibetan monk, and neo-Dzogchen educator and therapist. His work has been a central inspiration in the creation of the Open Path in many ways, especially in his teachings regarding fixations and deconstructive inquiry, and in his clear presencing of nondual awareness. I am also deeply grateful for the radical Dzogchen teachings of Keith Dowman and his brilliant translations of Dzogchen texts.

The classic Advaita teachers Ramana Maharshi and Sri Nisargadatta Maharaj, through their books, have been steady companions for many years, and their insights and methods of inquiry have also been formative in the style of the Open Path. The work of the great fourteenth-century Tibetan Dzogchen master Longchenpa has been pivotal for me, and is probably my most frequent source of inspiration. His work is complemented for me by the writings of many other Tibetan masters, Dakpo Tashi Namgyal (sixteenth century) in particular, as well as the profound tantras found in the book *The Supreme Source*. Another important teacher has been Jean Klein — traces of his insights and methods are to be found throughout this book. Further debts are owed to the teachings of Shabkar Lama, Tsoknyi Rimpoche, Chogyal Namkhai Norbu, Lex Hixon, John Daido Loori, John Wheeler, Adyashanti, Peter Francis Dziuban, Francis Lucille, Rupert Spira, and perhaps most of all, Jack Kerouac.

Acknowledgements

First and last and all the way through I want to thank my wife, Elizabeth Rabia Roberts, for her love, support, and inspiration during the creation of this book and the Open Path trainings from which it came. For years, our morning dialogues and inquiries were the proving ground where the material in these pages was tested and clarified. This book wouldn't exist without her insight and encouragement.

It also wouldn't exist without the financial support of the Sufi Way, and the spiritual friendships that are its reason for being. All my friends and students within the Way and in Open Path trainings have contributed to the creation of this book through their personal commitment to the art of awakening. Their clear presence, intelligence, humor, and good-heartedness were the context in which it grew. I would like to name all of you but the list would be too long, so please accept here my bow of thanks for every conversation, question, comment, telephone call, meditation, and prayer that we shared over these years. It has been a privilege to travel with you on this path.

Special thanks to Jeff Fuller, Carol Barrow, Amrita Skye Blaine, and Boudewijn Boom for much needed editorial help and suggestions, and to Connie Shaw of Sentient Publications for her belief in this project and the ease and professionalism with which she brought it into being.

Finally, I want to express my warmest gratitude to Melissa Stuart, John and Margo Steiner, Lynnaea and Rick Paine, Ginny Jordan, and Robert Gass for their friendship, guidance, and financial support during the years when the Open Path was born, and when Rabia and I were simultaneously venturing forth to places like Burma, Syria, Iraq, Iran, Pakistan, and Afghanistan. Your confidence in us, and your realization of the clear light of being, were a support beyond measure.

About the Author

Elias Amidon is the spiritual director (Pir) of the Sufi Way International, a non-sectarian mystical order in the lineage of Sufi Inayat Khan. An initiate of the Sufi Way for the past forty-three years, Pir Elias has studied with Qadiri Sufis in Morocco, Theravadan Buddhist teachers in Thailand, Native American teachers of the Assemblies of the Morning Star, Christian monks in Syria, Zen teachers of the White Plum Sangha, and contemporary teachers in the Dzogchen tradition.

Elias has lived a multifaceted, engaged life, working as a schoolteacher, carpenter, architect, writer, environmental educator, peace activist, and wilderness rites-of-passage guide. He helped develop several schools, including the Boulder Institute for Nature and the Human Spirit, the Institute for Deep Ecology, the graduate program in Environmental Leadership at Naropa University, and the Open Path. Co-editor of the books *Earth Prayers, Life Prayers,* and *Prayers for a Thousand Years,* he has worked for many years with his wife, Elizabeth Rabia Roberts, as a citizen activist for peace and interfaith understanding in Iraq, Syria, Afghanistan, Iran, Pakistan, and Israel/Palestine, and with indigenous tribes in Thailand and Burma on issues of cultural continuity and land rights (see: www.pathofthefriend.org). He was instrumental in founding the *Masar Ibrahim Al Khalil* (Abraham's Path), an international project dedicated to helping Middle Eastern countries open a network of cultural routes and walking trails throughout the region.

Pir Elias has been leading programs in Sufism for over three decades, and Open Path programs since 2005. Nine-month Open Path Trainings are offered frequently in the United States, England, Holland, and Germany. These trainings give participants a chance to work directly with Elias over an extended period, learning to recognize and sustain the freshness of nondual awareness in their lives. Week-long solitary Open Path retreats are also held frequently at Nada Hermitage in Crestone, Colorado.

Information about current Open Path programs can be found at www.open-path.org and at www.sufiway.org.

Sentient Publications, LLC publishes books on cultural creativity, experimental education, transformative spirituality, holistic health, new science, ecology, and other topics, approached from an integral viewpoint. Our authors are intensely interested in exploring the nature of life from fresh perspectives, addressing life's great questions, and fostering the full expression of the human potential. Sentient Publications' books arise from the spirit of inquiry and the richness of the inherent dialogue between writer and reader.

Our Culture Tools series is designed to give social catalyzers and cultural entrepreneurs the essential information, technology, and inspiration to forge a sustainable, creative, and compassionate world.

We are very interested in hearing from our readers. To direct suggestions or comments to us, or to be added to our mailing list, please contact:

SENTIENT PUBLICATIONS, LLC

1113 Spruce Street
Boulder, CO 80302
303-443-2188
contact@sentientpublications.com
www.sentientpublications.com